SOFT
FURNISHING

SOFT FURNISHING

A practical manual for
the home upholsterer

A. V. White

ROUTLEDGE & KEGAN PAUL
London, Boston and Henley

First published in 1956
This revised edition published in 1980
by Routledge & Kegan Paul Ltd
39 Store Street, London WC1E 7DD,
9 Park Street, Boston, Mass. 02108, USA and
Broadway House, Newtown Road,
Henley-on-Thames, Oxon RG9 1EN
Set in 10/11pt Linocomp Plantin by
Rowland Phototypesetting Ltd, Bury St Edmunds, Suffolk
and printed in Great Britain by
Whitstable Litho Ltd, Whitstable, Kent

British Library Cataloguing in Publication Data

White, Alice Violet

Soft furnishing. – Revised ed.
1. Drapery   2. Slip covers
3. Bedding   4. Upholstery
I. Title
646.2′12   TT387   79-41757

ISBN 0 7100 0550 4
ISBN 0 7100 0294 7 pbk

Contents

Metric conversion chart

$$3 \text{ mm} = \tfrac{1}{8} \text{ inch}$$
$$6 \text{ mm} = \tfrac{1}{4} \text{ inch}$$
$$10 \text{ mm} = \tfrac{3}{8} \text{ inch}$$
$$12 \text{ mm} = \tfrac{1}{2} \text{ inch}$$
$$15 \text{ mm} = \tfrac{5}{8} \text{ inch}$$
$$20 \text{ mm} = \tfrac{3}{4} \text{ inch}$$
$$22 \text{ mm} = \tfrac{7}{8} \text{ inch}$$
$$25 \text{ mm} = 1 \text{ inch}$$
$$23 \text{ cm} = \tfrac{1}{4} \text{ yard}$$
$$45 \text{ cm} = \tfrac{1}{2} \text{ yard}$$
$$70 \text{ cm} = \tfrac{3}{4} \text{ yard}$$
$$91 \text{ cm} = 1 \text{ yard}$$
$$1 \text{ metre} = 39\tfrac{1}{4} \text{ inches}$$

The illustrations in Fig. 33 (a-f) are included by kind permission of Rufflette Ltd.

Introduction

Soft furnishing is a fascinating subject and might be described as making the most out of our surroundings with the aid of fabrics.

The interior of a home is of interest to most of us whether pupil in the Home Economics Department or student in a bed-sitter, flat or house.

At some time or other we may find ourselves the occupier of a room with furniture and furnishings not to our liking. We may not be in a position to buy new furniture or alter what is already installed. Therefore the purchase of fabric is necessary, either to dress it up or hide it. Fabrics need not always be new; often very good quality drapes can be obtained in salerooms.

It is with this in mind that I have tried to give the basic information which will enable one to purchase suitable materials and make the necessary furnishings and to carry out many simple upholstery jobs.

Planning plays an important part in the furnishing of a home. It is not necessary to spend a lot of money; with a little care and forethought good, pleasing results can be obtained in interior decoration. Consideration should be given to the position of the room, its size, and the furniture it contains. There are many excellent books on this subject.

There is a large range of fabrics used in furnishings. These fabrics vary both in width and price, the more luxurious being the most costly. But this does not mean that the wearing properties are necessarily any better than those cheaper in price. Where the weave is more intricate and there is a mixture of fibres, the cost may be higher. Many large department stores, and some shops, specialise in furnishing fabrics, selling only fabrics manufactured by reputable firms. They employ sales staff who know a great deal about the fabrics they handle and are only too willing to help and guide the customer. Before making a purchase it is wise to consider how much wear and strain there is likely to be on the fabrics. Materials chosen for the making of loose covers will have to stand up to constant washing or cleaning and therefore should be of good quality and washable. (Note: the covers should be washed or cleaned before they get too dirty, otherwise the friction caused through hard rubbing of dirty parts when wet will gradually produce holes or shabby areas.)

CHAPTER 1
Basic processes

Throughout the whole of this book reference is made to this chapter, and it is in this section that the essential processes are given.

Soft furnishing requires larger stitches than are used by the fine needlewoman, because the materials are of a heavier quality.

Plain seams are used. These are first stitched by machine 8-10 stitches to 25 mm. The seam is pressed open and raw edges neatened by a large zig-zag stitch on a swing needle machine, or neatened by hand using oversewing or loop stitch. The stitches should be half the depth of the seam allowance.

The stitches

Tacking (Fig. 1) may be worked on the right or wrong side and from right to left. It is used to hold two or more pieces of fabric together before machining. Use long and short stitches alternately.

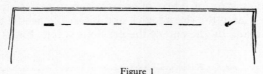

Figure 1

Running stitch (Fig. 2) Work from right to left; stitches and spaces are equal but should not be longer than 6 mm. Fasten on and off by working two back stitches (Fig. 2a and b).

1

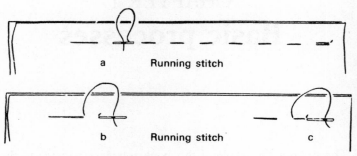

Figure 2

Gathering stitch (Fig. 3) is worked in the same way as running stitch, but the space is twice the length of the stitch.

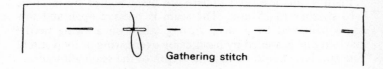

Figure 3

Back stitch (Fig. 4) Worked mostly on the wrong side of the fabric and used in place of machine stitching. Secure the thread as for running stitch. Work from right to left. Take up twice the amount of fabric in comparison to the size of stitch required. Carry the thread back and insert the needle through the hole made by the end of the previous stitch (Fig. 4).

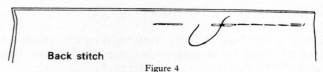

Figure 4

Loop stitch or *blanket stitch* (Fig. 5) Worked on the wrong side and used to neaten raw edges. Secure the thread by taking a few running stitches in the edge of fabric (Fig. 5a). The needle is placed into the fabric with point towards the worker and thread forming a loop under the point of the needle (Fig. 5b). Work from left to right. To fasten off run the needle through the fabric on the wrong side (Fig. 5d). The stitches are usually equal to half the depth of the turning.

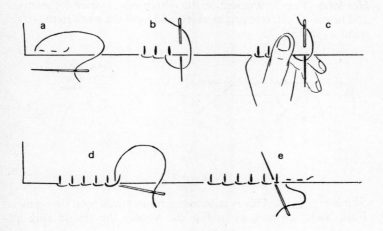

Figure 5

Oversewing (Fig. 6) May be used to join two edges together on the right side, but first turn under the raw edges. When used for neatening raw edges the stitches should be equal to half the depth of the turning.

Begin by bringing the needle out through the near piece of material and leave a short end; insert the needle at right angles to the edge and stitch over the short end (Fig. 6a and b). Fasten off by working two or three stitches together.

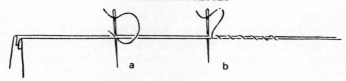

Figure 6

Hemming (Fig. 7) Worked on the wrong side, is used for seams and hems. Work from right to left and hold the work in the left hand as in Fig. 7c.

Figure 7

Slip hem (Fig. 8) This is an inconspicuous stitch used for hems. Fold back the hem as in Fig. 8a. Secure the thread with a

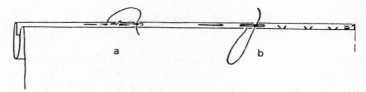

Figure 8

double back stitch, then pass the needle along the fold for 10 mm. Pick up two or three threads from the lower fabric (Fig. 8b).

4

Types of sewing threads

Tacking cotton A poor type of cotton obtainable on 1,000 yard reels at low cost. It is therefore economical to use in the preparation of work for machining.

Pure sewing silk is used for silk and woollen fabrics because it gives with the stretch of the fabric.

Cotton is obtainable in a wide range of colours and should be used for cotton fabrics.

Mercerised cotton is suitable for sewing rayons and may also be used for cotton fabrics and linen.

Synthetic thread is used for the making up of synthetic fabrics.

Buttonhole twist or *button thread* is very strong and is used where there is great strain, for example in the stitching in the centre of a sun button cushion.

Cutting and joining of crossway (bias) strips

1 Fold the material so that the selvedge threads lie along the weft thread as in Fig. 9a. Cut along the fold. This material is on the true cross and is similar to elastic; it will stretch to fit a curve or corner. When stretched it will not spring back to its original size and shape.

2 Make a paper marker to use as a guide so that the strips are of equal width. A-B is equal to width of binding, usually 25-40 mm (Fig. 9b).

3 Place edge of marker to the cut edge of fabric and slide along, chalk marking at the same time (Fig. 9c).

4 It is advisable to cut away the shaded portion as in Fig. 9d to ensure that all joins will run in the same direction.

5 All joins are made on the straight thread. Place the two right sides of strips together with the sharp points protruding as in Fig. 9e. Backstitch together and press seam open. Note that the stitching lies along a straight thread of both pieces of material.

6 Open out and press and then cut off the protruding points as the shaded portion of Fig. 9f shows.

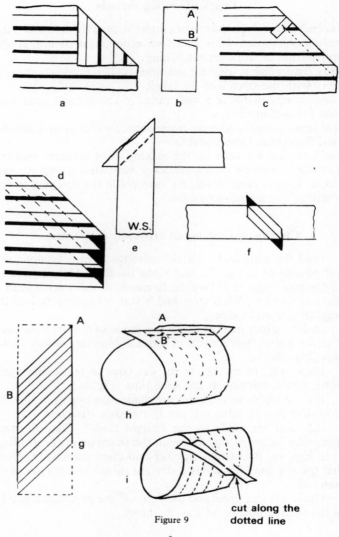

Figure 9

cut along the
dotted line

7 Crossway pieces. These pieces are used mostly for the covering of piping cord which is inserted between the joins of the fabric for decorative purposes, such as the seams of divan covers, loose covers for chairs, cushions, etc.

Note: When large quantities of crossway strips are required, i.e. for piping chair covers or divans, long narrow strips may be used (Fig. 9g). Fold back the top left-hand corner and cut on the cross; mark off the width of the strips, usually 40 mm for piping. Cut off the bottom right-hand corner (Fig. 9g). Pin point A to point B so that the seam begins on a drawn line and ends on one (Fig. 9h). Machine and open out the join. The joined piece will appear twisted (Fig. 9i). Cut along the dotted line and a long continuous strip, with all the pieces joined together, will be the result.

Piping

PIPING CORDS

Piping cord is obtainable in various thicknesses, from one- to three-ply or three-core cords.

Very fine This is never used for cushions as it is only the thickness of four-ply wool and is therefore suitable for eiderdowns.

Fine Two-core piping is sometimes used on cushions; it is about the thickness of quick-knit wool.

Medium Three-core piping is generally used for cushions, loose covers, etc.; it is either fawn colour or pure white and is 6 mm thick.

Coarse Three-core piping is used for a ruched border and is 12 mm thick.

THE PREPARATION FOR PIPING

All piping cord should be boiled so that it is completely shrunk and will not cause difficulty when laundered. The piping cord should be covered with crossway strips. This is done by placing the cord in the centre of the wrong side of the crossway strip and tacking close to the cord (Fig. 10a). A sufficient length of crossway strips should be prepared before the cord is inserted. Strips cannot be added easily while preparing the piping.

INSERTION OF PIPING

1 Tack the piping on the right side of the material, the raw edge of piping to the raw edge of the article (Fig. 10b).

2 When turning a corner, snip the piping down to the cord as in Fig. 10c and then turn the corner, keeping the corner square (Fig. 10c and d). Backstitch the piping at the corner.

3 To join a three-core piping cord, remove one strand from the left-hand piece and two strands from the right-hand piece. Twist the remaining three strands together and bind with cotton (Fig. 10e and f). An alternative is to splice them as in Fig. 11e. The material covering the cord should next be crossway-joined, thus forming a continuous covering of the cord.

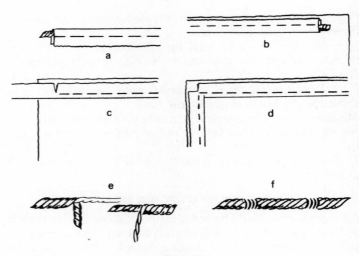

Figure 10

PIPING FOOT

Piping cannot be machined on to a piece of material without a piping foot. The ordinary foot of the machine should be removed and replaced with either an ordinary piping foot or an adjustable one. The cord can either be machined to the right of the foot or the left, by first altering an adjustable screw at the back of the foot.

Stitching on of decorative cords

1 Thread a medium-sized needle with cotton to match the cord; fasten on the thread by two or three overcasting stitches at the end where the cord is to be attached. Leave about 50 mm of cord extending beyond the edge where the thread has been secured.

2 Put the needle between one of the strands of the cord, pull through, then insert the needle into the material and take up about 5 mm (Fig. 11a) and continue stitching.

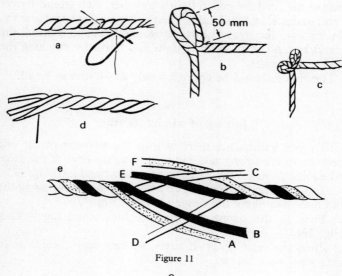

Figure 11

3   If the cord is attached to a loose cover for chair or bed, and a corner is to be turned, the braid is still stitched on as for an ordinary straight edge, but take an extra stitch at the very point of the corner to secure.

When turning a corner on a cushion cover, a fancy loop may be made by making a 50 mm loop (Fig. 11b); the cord is secured at the base of the loop. The top of the loop is brought down to the base and stitched (Fig. 11c).

Method 1   Unpick the seam near the end of the cord for about 25 mm, untwist the end of the cord (Fig. 11d) and insert into the seam, then secure the seam.
Method 2   Untwist both ends of the cord for a little way. Then place together so that the strands of the one end of the cord alternate between the strands of the other as in Fig. 11e. The ends of the cord are pulled tightly together. Pass strand B over E and under F and pull tight. Then take each strand separately, passing over the strand nearest to it, and going underneath the strand beyond. Pull all ends tight and finish by stitching the cord to the cover.

The splice should be approximately 25-40 mm in length.

Joining of widths together

1   To join widths together, turn in the selvedge of the one piece on to the wrong side and place over the edge of the piece to be joined. Match the pattern of the fabric and pin (Fig. 12a).
2   Slip-tack the two together, by slipping the needle along the fold and then along the single material (Fig. 12b).
3   Turn to the wrong side and machine along the tacking (Fig. 12c).
4   Press the seam open. If there is a raw edge, neaten as in methods 1 or 2 below.

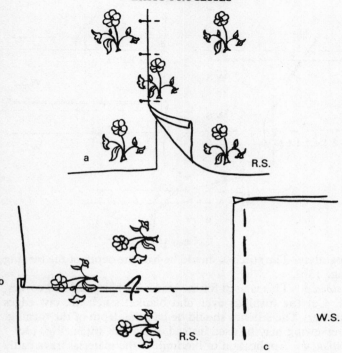

Figure 12

Neatening of raw edges

STITCHING OR BINDING

Use the zig-zag stitch on a swing-needle machine, or use one of the following methods:

Method 1 Used mostly for unlined curtains. Turn under the raw edge and hem like a run and fell seam (Fig. 13a).

Method 2 This method is used when an additional firm material is attached, e.g. frills, etc. Blanket stitch each edge

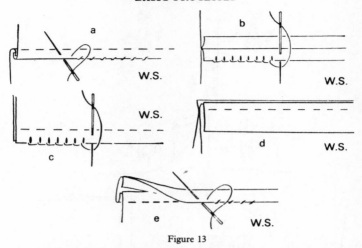

Figure 13

separately. The stitches should be half the depth of the turning (Fig. 13b).

Method 3   This is used for the seams of chairs and bed-covers, etc. Cut the turnings even and blanket stitch the raw edges together. The stitches should be half the depth of the turning. Oversewing may be used instead of blanket stitch (Fig. 13c).

Method 4   Application of binding. If the material frays badly then the edges should be bound. Place a strip of bias binding to the raw edge and machine 5 mm away from the edge (Fig. 13d). Turn the binding over the raw edge and hem (Fig. 13e).

FACINGS

These are used to neaten raw edges and are generally turned over on to the wrong side in soft furnishings. They may be used to lengthen curtains, bed-covers, etc. The hem of the article is first let down and pressed before the facing is applied.

1   Cut the facing on the straight of the material and to the depth required, usually 25-40 mm.

2   Place the right side of facing to the right side of the article, tack and machine 5 mm from the edge (Fig. 14a).

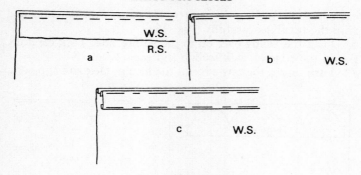

Figure 14

3 Press the turnings open. Turn the facings over on to the wrong side of article, bringing the join about 3 mm below the edge of the article. Tack firmly (Fig. 14b).

4 Turn under raw edge, tack (Fig. 14c) and slip hem (Fig. 8). Press.

Note: Bias binding may be used for facings. The binding can be purchased on cards, and is usually 12-25 mm wide.

SHAPED FACING

Sometimes a fancy-shaped edge is required on stools, bed-covers, etc. How to make a scalloped facing is shown here.

1 Make a template of the shape on stiff paper or cardboard. Mark round this shape on the wrong side of the article, using tailor's chalk for marking (Fig. 15a).

2 Cut out a piece of material the depth of the scallop plus 50 mm.

3 Place right side of facing to right side of the article and tack.

4 Turn the article over to the wrong side and tack carefully on the chalk lines, then machine (Fig. 15b). Turn the point of the scallop by leaving the machine needle in the material at the point; raise the presser bar and swivel the material into position for the next scallop.

5 Cut the surplus material away by cutting 5 mm away from

13

each scallop. At the point, snip to the edge of the stitching and
snip the turnings carefully (Fig. 15c).
6   Turn the facing over on to the wrong side. Tack carefully
round the edge of each scallop and press (Fig. 15d).
7   Turn under the raw edge of the facing, tack and slip hem.

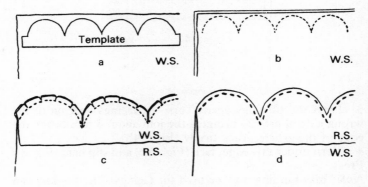

Figure 15

CHAPTER 2

Cushions, mattresses and quilting

Before the introduction of upholstered furniture, cushions were used on chairs and benches, the covers being made of embroidered fabrics. The size varied for long cushions from 122 × 46 cm to 76 × 46 cm, square cushions being between 46 cm and 76 cm square.

Cushions are used to give added colour to a room as well as additional comfort. Covers are made of either serviceable fabrics which will launder well or rich fabrics which can be dry-cleaned.

Cushion pads

A cushion pad is the inside of a cushion which is hidden by the cover; it may be made from the following materials.

Featherproof is a finely woven cotton fabric, specially treated to make it down-proof. It is used to make cushion pads when stuffed with down or feathers. The material is obtainable 142 cm wide.

Ticking is not such a closely woven fabric and is usually obtained in a twill weave, often striped. It is cheaper to purchase, is 142 cm wide and is used for feather fillings.

Calico is the name given to a plain cotton fabric and is used for cushion pads of kapok, latex crumbs, etc.

Fillings

Down is the best filling because it is soft, extremely fluffy and light in weight. It is obtained from geese, the breast feathers

15

only being used. For a cushion 50 cm square, ½-kilo of down would be required.

Feathers are graded into various qualities; the cheaper the grade, the coarser the feathers. They are sold in 1-kilo bags which are sufficient for a 50 cm square cushion.

Kapok is a fibre similar to cotton which is imported into this country. The soft, silky, cream-coloured fibre is very resilient, light in weight, buoyant and highly moisture-proof. Because of these qualities it is very valuable for stuffing. It should be picked over carefully by hand to fluff up before filling a cushion pad.

Latex foam is similar to a rubber sponge and is light in weight. It can be purchased already moulded into cushion shapes or into the shapes of quite a large variety of chair seats. It does not lose its shape during constant usage.

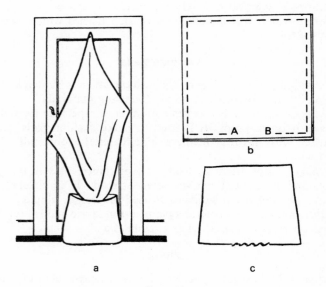

Figure 16

Foam crumbs are very small pieces of foam rubber which are sold in ½-kilo bags. The crumb is light in weight and very resilient.

Terylene filling and dacron fibrefill both look like very soft, springy cotton wool. They are hygienic because they can be washed, and they are also non-allergic.

Old eiderdowns Often the down from very old eiderdowns may be used for cushion pads. Unpick the stitching of the design and shake the feathers down to one corner. Have the down-proof case ready to put the feathers into. Drawing-pin three sides of the eiderdown to the back of a door, preferably an outside door. Place the cushion under the point of the eiderdown, cut a hole in the corner of the eiderdown and let the down fall into the case, as in Fig. 16a.

Cutting and making of cushion pad

1 Cut two pieces of material the size of the finished cushion plus 15 mm turnings on all sides. The choice of material depends upon the stuffing to be used. Make a cushion at least 46 cm square, unless it is for some particular chair, because a cushion looks small when filled.

2 Place the two right sides together and machine round the three sides and part of the fourth as in Fig. 16b. Use No. 40 cotton with a size 14 machine needle; 12 stitches to 25 mm.

3 Turn the cover to the right side and stuff carefully. Try to empty the down into the cushion pad rather than put a handful in at a time, otherwise the slightest draught will make the down fly about the room. Feathers do not fly so readily but should not be handled more than is necessary. Kapok should be picked over to separate some of the fibres and fluffed out before being put into the cushion pad. Push firmly into the corners. Stitch up opening by oversewing (Fig. 16c).

Note: Round, oval, square or oblong cushion pads of latex foam may be purchased already moulded to the required shape. These pads only need covering with calico. Instructions for making these covers have been given above.

17

Shaped cushion pads (patterns)

ROUND PADS

The measurement across a circle is known as the diameter and the measurement taken all the way round the circle is known as the circumference (Fig. 17a).

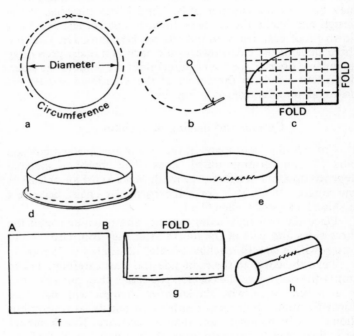

Figure 17

To draw a circle without a compass put a knot in the end of a piece of string. Place a drawing pin through the knot and secure to the centre of a sheet of paper. Tie a pencil half the diameter of the circle away from the drawing pin and draw the circle (Fig. 17b).

OVAL PADS

Cut an oblong-shaped sheet of paper and fold into four; divide this small oblong shape up into squares and draw in the curved shape at one corner (Fig. 17c). Cut through all four thicknesses of paper.

BOX CUSHION PADS

These may be round, square or oblong. Cut two pieces of material the size required for the top and bottom of the cushion. Cut a strip of material the depth required, from 50 to 110 mm. The length of the strip should be equal to the circumference plus 25 mm.

Method

1   Join the two ends of the strip together with a plain seam. Press the turnings open.

2   Place the right side of the strip to the right side of the cushion (Fig. 17d). Tack the two together 15 mm from the edge. Machine the two together.

3   Place the second piece of material to the opposite side of the strip and machine together, but leave an opening about 200 mm.

4   Turn the cushion right side out and stuff. Stitch up the opening as in Fig. 17e.

BOLSTER SHAPE PADS

1   Cut two circles of material the size required, also a piece of material the length of the bolster and equal in width to the circumference of the circles plus 15 mm at both sides (Fig. 17f).

2   Fold the material in two lengthways. Stitch as in Fig. 17g but leave the centre open.

3   Sew a circle at both ends of the casing.

4   Turn to the right side and stuff with feathers, hair or kapok.

5   Stitch up the opening (Fig. 17h).

Materials

Cushions may be made from all types of fabrics, including leather and tapestry. The thicker the material and the larger the design, the simpler the style of cushion cover should be.

Soft materials or thin furnishing fabrics suitable for cushions: silk, rayon, satin, taffeta, velvet, cretonne, linen, chintz.

Thick materials suitable for plain styles of cushion covers where there is no ruching or pleating: tweed, serge, corded nylon, damask, brocade, moquette, tapestry, corduroy, dralon, velour, leather, cotton and jute cloth.

Patterned materials Study the design carefully so that the main motif lies in the centre of the cushion shape. This may prove wasteful if the design is large but is the only way of obtaining a balanced and pleasing effect (Fig. 18).

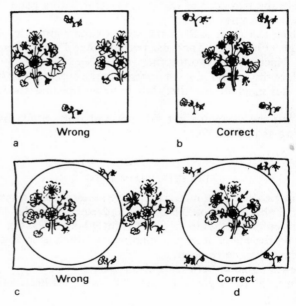

Figure 18

20

Fringed cushions

CHOICES OF MATERIAL

Loosely woven fabrics from which the threads can easily be withdrawn are the most suitable, such as folk-weaves, furnishing tweeds.

SUITABLE SHAPES

Square cushions with a fringed border on all four sides can easily be made; or oblong-shaped cushions with a fringe at either end (Fig. 19a and b).

CALCULATION OF MATERIAL

Measure the size of the cushion and add 60 mm (depth of fringe) on all four sides, i.e. a cushion 46 cm square with a 60 mm fringe would require two pieces of material 54 cm square (Fig. 19c). Total amount of material 70 cm of 122 cm width.

For an oblong cushion measure the size of the cushion and add 60 mm (depth of fringe) at both ends, i.e. a cushion 51 cm long × 38 cm wide would require a piece of material 65 cm × 38 cm. This is only for one side of the cover. Since the fringe is at the ends only, the cover can be cut out to a fold as in Fig. 19d. Allow 40 mm on the long side for opening (Fig. 19d).

METHOD OF MAKING FRINGED CUSHION (SQUARE)

1   Cut the two pieces of material by the straight thread of the fabric.
2   Machine along one side (single material) the depth of fringe from the edge (Fig. 19e). This is to prevent the fringe fraying beyond the calculated depth on the end to be left for the opening. Do this to both pieces of the cover.
3   Place the two wrong sides of cushion cover together. Tack the two together the depth of fringe from the edge, the tacking should be to a straight thread. Leave the fourth side open for the opening (Fig. 19f).

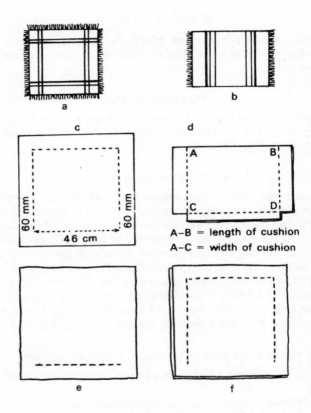

Figure 19

4 Machine along the tacking thread and again 3 mm inside this stitching, then fray out the threads to form a fringe on all four sides, so that the cushion cover looks like Fig. 19a.
5 Place the cushion inside the cover and stitch up the opening.

METHOD OF MAKING FRINGED CUSHION (OBLONG)

1 Cut one piece of material by a straight thread (Fig. 19d).
2 Fold the material in two and tack the two pieces of material, wrong sides together, the depth of fringe from the edge. Continue as for a square fringed cushion.

Plain piped cushion

CHOICE OF MATERIAL

A firm material should be used and not a thick one because the piping would be thick and bulky. Plain or patterned materials can be used with matching or contrasting piping.

SUITABLE SHAPES

Any shaped cushion may have a plain piped cover: round, square, oval, oblong, kidney, heart, etc.

CALCULATION OF MATERIAL

Two pieces of material are required, one for the top and one for the bottom, with 25 mm turnings on all sides. You also need sufficient crossway strips to go round the cushion.

METHOD

1 Cover medium three-core piping cord with crossway strips (Fig. 10a).
2 Tack the fold of the piping 25 mm from the edge of the cover. Snip the material at the corners, as shown in Fig. 20a.
3 Place the two right sides of the cover together and tack round three sides (Fig. 20b).
4 Machine, using a piping foot. Machine the piping to the openings separately.
5 Cut the turnings to 10 mm and cut off the corners and blanket stitch as Fig. 20c. These stitches are quite large, i.e. equal to half the depth of the turning, or zig-zag stitch on the machine.

23

6 Turn the cover right side out. Make the opening as Fig. 28a (p. 40). Press.

7 Place in the cushion pad and fasten the fasteners.

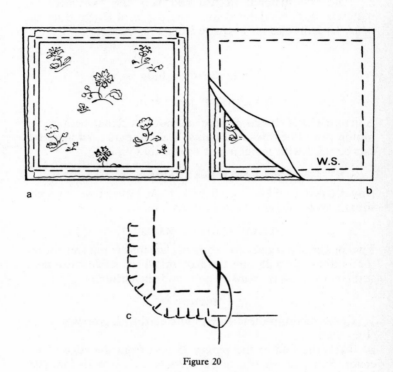

Figure 20

Box cushions

CHOICE OF MATERIALS

Box cushions can be made from firm curtain fabrics or thick tapestry. The thicker the material the plainer the style of cushion should be, i.e. a thin material is suitable for box cushions with either a gathered or pleated panel round the sides; thick tapestry can only be made into box cushions with a straight panel round the sides.

SUITABLE SHAPES

There are a variety of shapes for box cushions, including square, round, oval and semi-circular. The depth of the panel round the sides can vary from 50 to 100 mm when finished, according to the size and purpose of the cushion. If the cushion is to be used for the seat of a chair, a panel of 100 mm should be used.

CALCULATION OF MATERIAL

For box cushions, two pieces of material the size of the cushion pad plus 15 mm on all sides are required and a strip of material the depth of the finished panel plus 15 mm on either side for turnings. The length of strip should be equal to the circumference of the cushion pad (this is the measurement taken all the way round the cushion pad) plus 25 mm for the join.

METHOD

1 Cover a medium three-core piping cord, with crossway strips (details on Fig. 10a).

2 Tack the piping to the right side of the cushion as for a square cushion (Fig. 20a). Do this to both top and bottom pieces.

3 Join the side band with a plain seam, placing the two right sides together and machining 15 mm from the edge. Press the turning open (Fig. 21a and b).

4 Attach the right side of the side band to the right side of the cushion. Snip the turnings of the side band at the corners. Tack firmly, then machine, using a fairly large machine stitch (Fig. 21c).

5 Attach the bottom of the cushion cover to the side band in the same way, but leave one whole and two half sides open (Fig. 21d).

6 Turn the right side out and press.

7 Place the cushion pad inside the cover and pin (Fig. 21e),

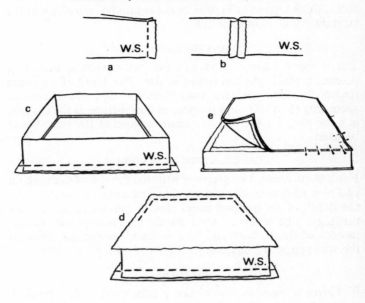

Figure 21

and stitch up the opening by slip hemming. Make sure that the corners of the top of the cushion match those of the underside.

Sun button cushions

CHOICE OF MATERIALS

Only soft furnishing fabrics that will gather easily can be used. The material may be plain or patterned. The sun button cushion is a type of cushion that has a padded centre from which gathers or pleats radiate. This centre panel may be quilted if a plain material is used. If a floral fabric is used, a large flower or spray of flowers in the centre makes an attractive cushion.

SUITABLE SHAPES

There are a variety of shapes, including square, round, and oval (Fig. 22a, b, c). The depth of the panel round the sides should be at least 80 mm and not more than 110 mm.

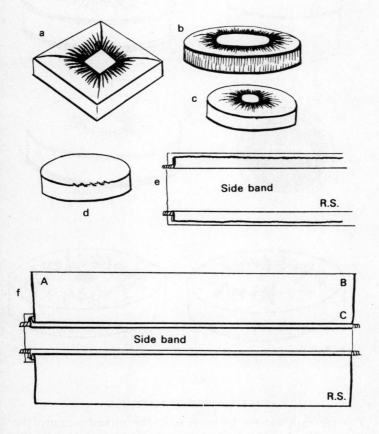

Figure 22 (a-f)

27

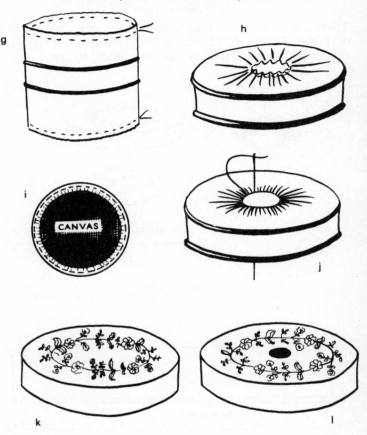

Figure 22 (g-l)

CALCULATION OF MATERIAL

Two pieces of material are required for the top and bottom of the cover. The length of these pieces should be equal to the circumference of the cushion plus 15 mm (A to B of Fig. 22f).

28

The depth of these strips should be equal to half the diameter of the cushion minus 40 mm (B to C of Fig. 22f). The depth of the band of the cushion should be 80-100 mm plus 15 mm turnings on either side. The length should be equal to the circumference plus 15 mm at either end. For example, a cushion pad 46 cm in diameter with a depth (side band) of 90 mm would require 70 cm of 122 cm material or 1.20 metres of 76 cm material. A length of medium-sized piping cord equal to twice the circumference of the cushion plus 80 mm for joining is required, and sufficient crossway strips to cover the piping cord.

METHOD

1   Cover the piping cord with material (Fig. 10a).
2   Tack the piping to the top and bottom edges of the side band (Fig. 22e).
3   Tack the top and bottom pieces of the cover to the side band (Fig. 22f).
4   Machine, using a piping foot.
5   Join A and B together to form a side seam. Join piping cord and crossway strip (Fig. 10f).
6   Place gathering thread in top and bottom. These stitches must not be small (Fig. 22g).
7   Place the cushion pad (Fig. 22d) inside the cover. Draw up the gathering thread as in Fig. 22h.
8   Cut two circles of material 130-50 mm in diameter, turn in the raw edges to the wrong side and tack. If the material is not firm, cut a circle of canvas and turn the raw edge of the material on to the canvas (Fig. 22i).
9   Tack the circle to the centre of the cushion top and bottom separately and hem.
10   With a large needle and matching thread, sew the two small circles together, pulling the thread very tight (Fig. 22j).
Note: A type of sun button cushion may be made without any gathers (Fig. 22k). For this, cut two circles of material for the top and bottom, and a strip of material for a side band; make

29

up as for box cushion (Fig. 21). Cut out small circles of cardboard about 40-50 mm in diameter and cover with contrasting material. Stitch buttons into position (Fig. 22l) and then stitch right through the cushion, as in Fig. 22j.

Round panel cushion

CHOICE OF MATERIAL

Firm materials may be used if the cushion is to have a straight band with either a corded or piped edge (Fig. 23a). If the material is firm but not thick, a pleated band may be used for the side of the cushion, or if the material is soft then a gathered border looks attractive.

CALCULATION OF MATERIAL

Two pieces of material are required for the top and bottom of the cushion cover plus 15 mm turnings all round. A strip of material the depth required plus 15 mm on either side should be cut, its length being equal to the circumference of cushion plus 25 mm for the join. If a gathered side band is wanted, allow 1½ times the circumference of the cushion. For pleats allow two to three times the length of the circumference of the cushion, according to the size of pleats.

METHOD

1 Tack round each circle separately 15 mm from the edge (Fig. 23b). This is to prevent the circle from stretching and the stitching of the cushion becoming uneven and so spoiling its round appearance.
2 Join up the side band and press the turnings flat.
3 Tack the right side of the side band to the right side of the cushion and machine (Fig. 23c).
4 Tack the bottom of the cushion cover to the side band but only machine three-quarters of the way round.
5 Turn the cover to right side out and press.

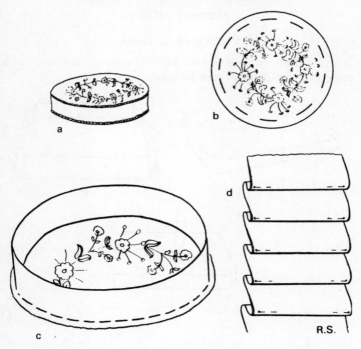

Figure 23

6 Stitch on a silk cord if the cover is made of silk, or a cotton cord if the cover is of cotton. Details of stitching were shown in Fig. 11.

7 Place the cushion pad inside the cushion cover and stitch up the opening by slip hemming.

Note: If a piping is used it should be tacked to the top and bottom sections of the cushion cover before the side band is attached. If a pleated panel is used for the side band, the pleats should be pinned carefully (Fig. 23d) and pressed before attaching to the cushion.

31

Mattress cushions

CHOICE OF MATERIAL

A thick firm material is best for this type of cushion, but a cotton or silk damask may be used.

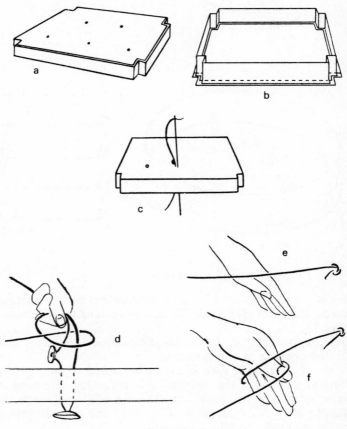

Figure 24 (a-f)

SUITABLE SHAPES

The shape of the cushion depends on the style of chair. Since a mattress cushion is a very firm type of cushion, it is used for window-seats and for the seats of some styles of chair. A paper pattern should be made of the exact shape of the seat, Fig. 24a. Should a new mattress be required and not just a cover then a deep pad of latex foam or firm synthetic foam should be purchased and cut to the required shape. This pad may be covered in a thin, plain cotton fabric and the cover is made like the outer cover minus the piping.

CALCULATION OF MATERIAL

Two pieces of material are required for top and bottom of cover. Allow 20 mm in every 250 mm for buttoning and 15 mm for turnings. A strip of material will be required for the side band, its depth being equal to the depth of the mattress pad, plus 30 mm for seams, and equal in length to the circumference of mattress plus 25 mm for joins. You also need sufficient crossway strips 40 mm wide to go round the cushion twice, plus joins.

METHOD

1 Cover medium-sized piping cord with the crossway materials. Details are shown in Fig. 10.
2 Tack the piping to the right side of cushion. Snip the piping at the corners. Details are shown in Fig. 10.
3 Attach the right side of the band to the right side of the cushion, snip the turnings at the corners (Fig. 24b). Tack firmly, then machine.
4 Attach the bottom of the cover in the same way, but leave open the widest side and part of the two shorter sides. Turn the cover right side out and press.
5 Place the pad inside the cover. Turn under the raw edge of the bottom section and pin carefully to the side band. Check to see that there is no puckering and that the corners are well shaped. Then join together. If the material is very strong it might be easier to use a semi-circular needle.

6   Mark the position of the buttons on both upper and under side of cushion to form a diamond pattern. The rows of buttons can vary from 100 to 150 mm apart, and the buttons 200 to 250 mm apart. These measurements are not rigid but simply give an idea of spacing.

7   Thread a mattress needle with twine, insert at the required position, pull through, then thread a covered button on to the needle and return about 5 mm from the point of insertion and thread on another button (Fig. 24c). A slip-knot is made with the twine as in Fig. 24d. The twine is then pulled tight so that the button will sink into the cushion. A secure knot is made in the twine before cutting off. This is done by putting the long end of twine in the right hand. Wrap it twice round the left hand, gradually open the thumb and fingers, grasp the small end of twine and pull through the loop. Let the twine slip off the fingers and pull tight with right hand (Fig. 24e and f).

MATTRESS TUFTS

These should be replaced as soon as it is noticed that they are missing. A mattress needle threaded with twine is inserted through the mattress and returned 15 mm away from the point of insertion. A slip-knot is made with the twine as in Fig. 24d, then a tuft, either leather, wool, or cotton is passed under the knot and under the loop of twine on the other side. The twine is then securely knotted and cut off.

English quilting

CHOICE OF MATERIAL

Thin materials only are suitable, such as rayon, silk, satin or glazed chintz. Use plain or patterned materials.

SUITABLE SHAPES

Any shaped cushion may have a quilted cover.

CALCULATION OF MATERIAL

Two pieces of material are required for the top and bottom of the cushion. The material should be the size of the cushion pad plus 15 mm turnings on all sides. Odd scraps of the same material will be required for covering the piping cord. One piece of muslin will also be required for lining the cushion. This should be the same size as the cushion cover.

METHOD

1   If using a plain fabric, then purchase a design for English quilting.
2   Place the shiny side of the transfer on to the muslin and pin carefully so that it is perfectly flat. Use a warm iron and iron all over the paper. Lift one corner of the transfer to make sure that the design has been transferred on to the muslin. If it has not taken then use a warmer iron.
3   Place a sheet of wadding on the wrong side of the silk and lay the muslin on top. Tack through firmly as in Fig. 25a.
4   Running stitch is used to hold all the thicknesses together permanently. Stem stitch is sometimes used if a solid line is required. The design on the paper may be tacked on to the wrong side of the cushion and then all the layers may be machined.
5   Make the cover up as for square cushion (Fig. 20).

a

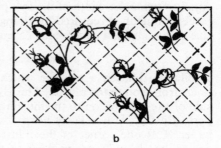
b

Figure 25

6   It is best to stitch the cover on to the cushion instead of having an opening and patent fasteners.

Note: Glazed chintz or patterned fabric (do not use a thick material) look very pretty when quilted. The whole of the surface may be covered with a diamond pattern quilting as in Fig. 25b or the design of the flowers outlined in stitching.

Italian quilting

CHOICE OF MATERIAL

Thin materials only are suitable for Italian quilting, such as good quality rayon, silk or satin. The fabric should not have a pattern of any kind but be perfectly plain.

SUITABLE SHAPES

Any shaped cushion may have a quilted cover.

CALCULATION OF MATERIAL

Measure the size of the cushion pad and allow 25 mm on all sides for turnings. Two pieces of material will be required, one for the top and the other piece for the bottom of the cover. If a frill is to be used round the sides of the cushion, a strip of material 1½ to 2 times the length of the circumference of the cushion will be required and the width of the strip should be equal to twice the width of the frill plus 15 mm turnings. One piece of muslin is required for lining the cushion of the same size as the cushion cover, plus 25 mm turnings.

METHOD

1   Having chosen a transfer which is composed of double lines, iron it on to the muslin. This is done by placing the shiny side of the transfer on to the muslin. Pin carefully so that it is perfectly flat. Use a fairly warm iron and iron all over the paper. Lift one corner of the transfer to make sure that the design has been transferred on to the muslin. If it has not taken, then use a warmer iron.

2   Place the muslin on to the wrong side of the silk (Fig. 26a).
Tack the muslin and silk together as for English quilting
(Fig. 25).

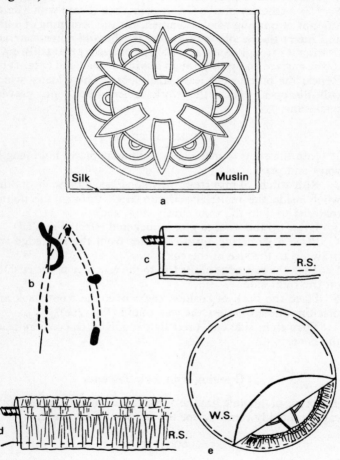

Figure 26

37

3   All the lines must be carefully worked in running stitch or machined. The stitches should look even on the right side.

4   Remove all tacking threads.

5   Use a tapestry needle (blunt point) and thread with a small amount of quilting wool. Commence at the beginning of a line and insert the needle between the muslin and outer material, passing it through as far as the shape or angle permits. Bring it to the surface and pull through leaving a small end (Fig. 26b). Repeat the process but leave small loops. These loops, which will disappear when the work is smoothed out, prevent puckering.

MAKING OF FRILL

1   Join the strip to make one continuous piece. Fold lengthways and press.

2   Run-stitch 10 mm from the fold. Place a piece of quilting wool inside the material and run-stitch through the double material to hold the wool firmly (Fig. 26c).

3   Draw up the wool to give a puckered effect (Fig. 26d).

4   Place a gathering thread 10 mm from the raw edge and draw up to the size of the cushion.

5   Tack the raw edge of the frill to the raw edge of the cushion on the right side.

6   Place the back of cushion cover over the front, tack and machine three-quarters the way round (Fig. 26e).

7   Turn right side out, press lightly and stitch cushion inside the cover.

Opening with a zip fastener

This type of opening has the one great advantage that the cover can be quickly removed for the purpose of laundering.

METHOD

1   Leave one side of the cover open for approximately three-quarters of its total length, i.e. a cover 54 cm in length would

require an opening of 38 cm, therefore a zip of that length is used.

2　The raw edge of the opening is turned under once and pressed. Unfasten the zip. Place the fold of the material to the edge of the teeth of the zip fastener and tack the depth of the teeth away from the edge (Fig. 27). Tack on to the back of the cover in the same way.

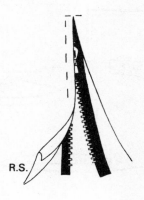

Figure 27

3　It is advisable to stitch the zip in by hand because its position makes the use of a machine difficult. The hand stitch used should be backstitch but the needle must be stabbed through the fabric, as owing to the thickness of the cover and the zip it will not be possible to backstitch the two together. Neaten the raw edges on the wrong side with blanket stitch.

Continuous strip opening

The length of the opening should be approximately three-quarters the length of one side.

METHOD

1 Cut a crossway strip of material twice the length of the opening and 40 mm wide.

2 With the cushion on the wrong side, snip the turnings at the ends of the opening down to the machine stitching (Fig. 28a). Turn the cover over on to the right side and bring out the turnings of the opening (Fig. 28b).

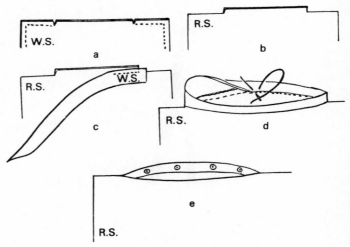

Figure 28

3 Place the right side of the strip to the right side of the cover and tack in line with the seam. The strip should be stitched all the way round the opening, then machined (Fig. 28c).

4 Turn under the raw edge of the strip and tack to the machine stitching of the strip on the inside of the cover, then hem (Fig. 28d).

5 The strip of material applied on the opening is tucked inside the cover and the opening is pressed. Stitch on patent fasteners 50 mm apart (Fig. 28e). Velcro or snap-fastener tape may also be used.

CHAPTER 3

Curtains, fittings, pelmets and blinds

A bare window-frame gives a room a severe appearance and does not permit privacy, so furnishing fabrics are used to give a softening effect and keep out draughts. It is best to line draw-curtains as this helps to preserve the curtains. The best lining is Milium, which looks like ordinary lining on one side, with a silvery sheen on the other. It is this insulating property which prevents heat loss in the winter and on a hot day keeps out the heat, thus virtually eliminating curtain-fading. The metallic side of Milium is the wrong side and the right side can be obtained in a wide range of colours. Always dry-clean this type of lining. The cost of Milium is only slightly higher than ordinary sateen lining, but it is worth the extra expense. Double-glazing is good, but triple-glazing is best for large windows; therefore money is wisest spent on good quality curtains and lining, even having an interlining on thin fabrics, which gives a padded effect and is useful for floor-length curtains.

Curtain fittings

There is a wide selection of fittings and many of these look attractive without pelmets or valances. The rail may be simple in design (Fig. 29a), and if a decorative curtain heading such as in Fig. 33a or 33d is used then the rail is completely hidden when the curtains are drawn. The rail (Fig. 29b) may fit flush to the underside of the lintel.

A decorative curtain track as in Fig. 29c may be used but

this depends upon the decor of the room. A track may have a cord attachment so that the curtains can be drawn without handling and a track for net curtains can also be attached at the same time (Fig. 29d).

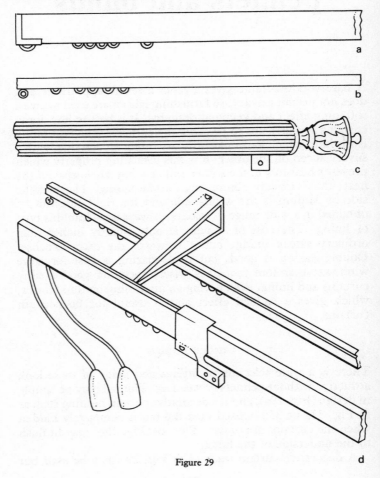

Figure 29

42

The design of tracks varies considerably and many developments are taking place. It is advisable to look at the displays in the departmental stores or the shops which specialise in these fittings.

If heavy curtains are to be used over a large space, then check the strength of the track for such a weight by asking for advice at the store before finally purchasing.

TO GIVE HEIGHT TO A WINDOW

Secure a piece of wood above the window-frame. The track, from which the curtains and frill hang, is attached to this. The pelmet or frill should be deep enough to hide the frame of the window (A to B, Fig. 30a).

TO WIDEN A WINDOW

Attach blocks of wood at either end of the window-frame and extend the track on to the shaded portions, Fig. 30b.

TO GROUP WINDOWS

If two (Fig. 30d) or three windows are close together in a room, group them by attaching a piece of wood at A, Fig. 30c, and between the windows at B and C. The track can be secured across the grouped frames (Fig. 30c).

The pelmet should be shaped so that the two windows form a complete unit (Fig. 30e).

Fabrics suitable for curtains

There is a very wide range of materials suitable for curtains and the choice of fabric may depend upon the furnishing of a room – antique or contemporary – and also the use for which the room is used – kitchen, or lounge, etc. The fabric may be man-made or natural and one should ask for advice from the sales representative in the store because the constant developments in fibres means that one cannot keep abreast of such developments. A brief list of some of the fabrics is given.

Cotton (91-183 cm wide)   May be in a plain weave or a satin.

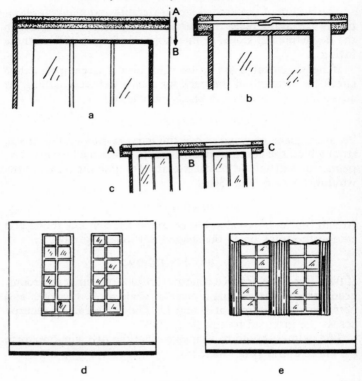

Figure 30

The latter is smooth to the touch and more expensive. It is strong, hard-wearing and easily laundered, but usually shrinks, although some fabrics are pre-shrunk. Colours are not always fast to sunlight, but again some fabrics are guaranteed. Fabrics may have a printed design on them and even the most expensive of these may be printed off the grain, which makes the matching of the fabric difficult, if the curtain is to hang properly. Sunlight and dust over a period of years can cause the fabric to rot.

Cretonne (122 cm wide) This is a reasonably priced fabric with a shadowy flowered pattern. It is very hard wearing and washes well; suitable for curtains and loose covers.

Cotton brocade (122 cm wide) More expensive and a heavier type of cotton suitable for more formal rooms.

Terry towelling (91 cm wide) May be purchased in a wide range of patterns. It is ideal for bathrooms because it will absorb the steam and help to lessen condensation. The printed pattern is inclined to wash out and fade.

Repp (122 cm wide) A reasonably priced fabric which is hard-wearing and suitable for curtains and loose covers. The fabric has a definite slubbed texture.

Velvet and velours (122 cm wide) These fabrics can be obtained with a plain or ribbed pile and also in a wide range of beautiful colours. The more subtle the colour the more expensive the fabric. They are suitable for formal rooms and also make good door curtains as they are heavy and help to keep out draughts. They should be made with the pile going downwards so that they do not catch and hold the dust. They should also be lined to prevent fading, and should be dry-cleaned. Check carefully when making up that the panels smooth downwards, because one panel made a different way could change the shade.

PVC-coated cottons (91 cm wide) These can be obtained shiny or matt finish, plain or patterned. The fabric is coated with transparent plastic film. It is ideal for shelf curtains and cushions for garden or beach. Can be sponged clean.

Rayon fabric (120 cm wide or wider) These fabrics can be obtained in heavy brocaded types or lightweight, often made of a mixture of cotton and rayon to make them stronger. They are inclined to fray easily and therefore greater care is required when making up. They will wash, but are often dry-cleaned. These fabrics are most attractive and are reasonably priced.

Nylon fabrics (120-83 cm wide) Usually made in a brushed nylon form in very rich colours. The fabric is bonded to a white tricel backing and has the appearance of velvet. It can be washed. Make up with pile going all in the same direction.

Fibreglass (122 cm wide) This is a lightweight, silky and slightly translucent fabric which can be obtained in delightful printed designs. It looks rich and luxurious but should not be lined because it would lose its translucent property. It is flame-proof and is useful for curtains near to cookers. Washes easily and drip-dries. It will not shrink, but should not be machine-washed. It frays badly and should be machined using fibreglass thread with a fine needle and large stitch – about 8 to 25 mm.

Plastic sheeting (91-122 cm wide) Semi-transparent and waterproof, it is therefore used for shower curtains. Can be obtained in a variety of designs and textures. Sponge clean and wipe dry.

Hessian (69-183 cm wide) Obtainable in a wide range of colours, it has a coarse texture. Suitable for a wall hanging, but the colours are not very fast.

Curtain lining (122 cm wide, maybe wider) Generally has a slightly satin weave and is sold in a wide range of colours, cream being the most popular. Milium lining can be used for curtains. It is a fabric coated with aluminium which acts as an insulator. It keeps out the heat in the summer and the cold in winter. It is slightly more expensive.

Roller blind fabric (76-259 cm wide) Strong, glazed fabric, plain or patterned.

STRIPED CURTAINS

Do not measure the length required off the roll of material, fold it back, cut the curtains and make up. The results might be the same as in Fig. 31a. Cut out each curtain separately and match the stripes so that the finished results will be as in Fig. 31b. Do not have horizontal stripes in a room that has a low ceiling, because this will make the room appear very low. Do not use a vertical stripe if the ceiling is high because this will make the window look very slender and the ceiling high.

PATTERNED FABRICS

Essential to the correct cutting of patterned fabrics is the arrangement of curtain widths in such a manner as will give a

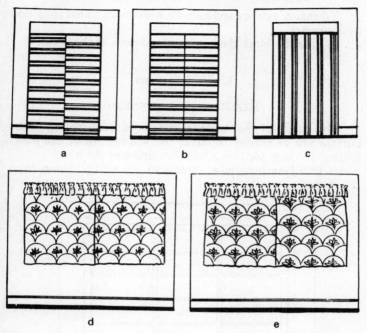

Figure 31

natural continuity of design throughout. Properly arranged, they will appear to be woven in a single width (Fig. 31b and c). If the material has a small repeat pattern as in Fig. 31d, see that both curtains are alike and the pattern is continuous across the window (Fig. 31d), otherwise a pair of horrible looking curtains may be made as in Fig. 31e. Flowers must grow upwards.

CURTAINS

Curtains are used chiefly for three reasons:
(a) To keep out draughts.

47

(b) To ensure privacy and give the window an added attraction by draperies.

(c) to hide the bleak darkness and coldness of the night.

Unlined curtains

MEASUREMENTS REQUIRED

1 The length of the curtain is measured from the top of the curtain rail or runner to either the window-sill or the floor, adding 150 mm for the curtain heading and the hem.

Note: Full-length curtains should always be 10-15 mm from the floor.

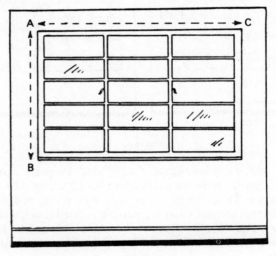

Figure 32

2 The width of the curtain should be 1½ times the width of the window A-C (Fig. 32). This allows for fullness and overlap, using standard heading tape. If pencil pleating tape is used (Fig. 33a), allow 2½ times the width of the window. The ends

48

of the tape are drawn up to form the pleats, Fig. 33b, and the hooks slipped into the pockets about every 80 mm, Fig. 33c. If using pinch-pleating tape (Fig. 33d), allow twice the width of window; these pleats are made by drawing up the cords (Fig. 33e) and inserting the special hooks which hold the pleats (Fig. 33f).

When using pleating heading tapes use a decorative pole or

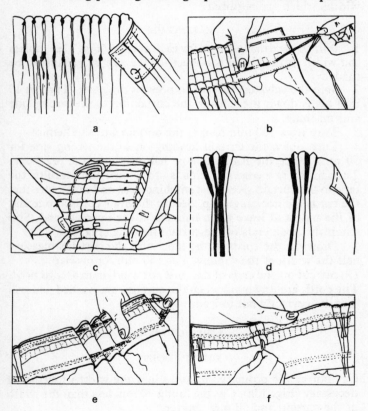

Figure 33

ceiling fixed track. If uncertain about this, make enquiries from the soft furnishing department of any large store.

CUTTING OUT

Cut off the first length of fabric the required size, keeping the threads straight, both top and bottom. Match the pattern of the fabric before cutting out the second width and any other widths which are required.

MAKING UP

1 Join the widths together for each curtain (Fig. 12a), unless the width of the fabric is correct for the size of curtains to be made.
2 Snip the selvedge threads to prevent dragging. Turn in 10 mm hems down the sides of the curtain on to the wrong side and machine.
3 Turn up a 100 mm hem at the bottom and slip hem.
4 Turn down the curtain heading on to the wrong side for 50 mm. Place the Rufflette tape half-way over the raw edge. Turn in the raw edge at the ends of the tape and machine the tape to the curtain. Keep the stitching even and make sure that the cords are not caught up. Secure the draw cords at one end of the tape and leave them hanging at the opposite end. Slip stitch the open ends of the curtain heading (Fig. 34a).
5 Draw up the cords in the tape until the curtains measure half the width of the window plus 150 mm for overlap.
Do not cut off the ends of the cord but wind on to a 'cord tidy'. The cords are unwound when the curtains are washed and will then be perfectly flat to iron.

Lined curtains

CUTTING OUT

Cut out as for ordinary curtains. Join the widths together if necessary (Fig. 12a). Cut the lining 30 mm less than the width of the curtain and 50 mm shorter.

MAKING UP

1   Turn in single hems on the sides of the curtain 30-40 mm wide and tack firmly (Fig. 34b). Snip the selvedges.

2   Turn up a 100 mm hem at the bottom of the curtain and fold under the corners (Fig. 34c). (If the material is very thick mitre the corners as for a pelmet.) Slip hem the hem of the curtain.

3   Place the wrong side of the lining to the wrong side of the curtain. Fold back one-third of the width of the lining and lock stitch the lining to the curtain (Fig. 34d). Commence the stitch 230 mm up from the bottom of the curtain and work from left to right, keeping the thread parallel to the fold of the lining. *Lock stitch:* Take the needle through about two threads of the lining and curtain fabric, place the cotton round the needle as in Fig. 34e, pull the needle through and tighten up the thread, thus locking the curtain and lining together. The stitches may be 30 mm apart.

The lock stitch is used to prevent the lining and the curtain puckering, the stitches must not show on the right side. Fold back the remaining one-third of the lining and lock stitch. If the curtains are wide the rows of lock stitch should be about 46 cm apart.

4   Turn in a single turning on the sides of the lining and tack to the curtain. Turn up a separate hem on the bottom of the lining and slip hem. This should be left free and not attached to the curtain.

5   Hem down the sides of the lining, catching it to the curtain. Backstitch the lining to the curtain at the corners (Fig. 34f).

6   Turn down the curtain heading at the top for 50 mm and place the Rufflette tape half over the raw edge of the curtain. Turn under the raw edge of the tape at the ends and machine. Secure the cords in the tape at one end and draw them up at the opposite end until the curtain is equal to half the window space, plus 150 mm.

Note: If a pelmet or valance is used with the curtains, a 25 mm curtain heading should be used instead of a 50 mm heading.

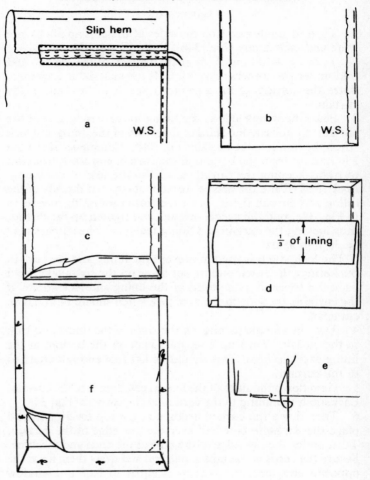

Figure 34

Detachable linings

These can easily be made and added to existing curtains as well as new ones.

The lining may be the size of the curtain or 1½ times the width of a pleated curtain (if pleated heading tape is used).

1 Join up the necessary width and sew the side hems. At the top use lining tape, which is specially designed for detachable linings.

2 Pull out the two cords and knot together at one end of the tape. Place the raw edge of the lining between the two 'skirts' of the lining tape with cord side uppermost. The tape should be slightly longer than the fabric so that it overlaps and this section can be turned under. Machine along the bottom of the tape thus trapping the lining between the two skirts.

3 Pull up the cords to correct size of curtain. Secure the ends of tape on a cord tidy. Place hooks in the tape 80 mm apart, then attach to tape of curtain.

The edges of the lining and curtain may be anchored together with a few tacks or a running thread if desired.

Portières (door curtains)

These are generally used in doorways to prevent draughts and also to obscure the unevenness of the door.

When used behind the doors, the fittings are so made that they are attached to the door-frame on the hinged side and on to a bracket fitting to the door opening. There are numerous types of fittings and advice as to the best type can be obtained from a good furnishing store. The fabric used for the curtain itself is of the heavier variety, such as chenille, velour, etc. It may be lined if desired and should be made up as for ordinary curtains, allowing extra width and length so that the curtain touches the floor.

Net curtains

These are semi-transparent. For town houses they are used a great deal where the outlook is ugly and where there is no privacy. The curtains may completely cover the window with a rod threaded through top and bottom slots (Fig. 35a), which helps to keep the curtains taut and prevents them from blowing about and getting torn when the windows are open.

The curtains may have frills down the sides (Fig. 35b). They may overlap at the bottom and be draped back at the sides (Fig. 35c). There should always be more than one set of casement curtains as they soil very quickly and require washing frequently.

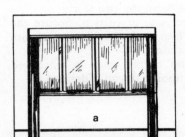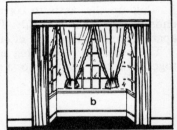

Figure 35 (a-c)

54

SUITABLE MATERIALS

The more transparent the material the better, so that it does not darken the room too much. The most suitable materials, therefore, are curtain ninon, nylon, net, transparent terylene etc.

These curtains are suspended from either rods or plastic-coated expanding wires. Some nets are suspended from curtain tracks. The choice depends upon the style of curtain; for example, if the curtains are to be held taut as in Fig. 35a then a rod or wire is used.

CALCULATION OF MATERIALS

Decide upon the style and whether to have a heading at the top and bottom. Take the measurements of the height required and add on to this twice the depth of the hem at the top and

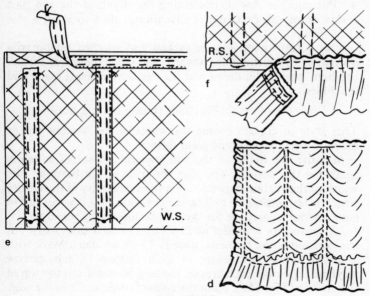

Figure 35 (d-f)

bottom, e.g. for a window 92 cm in height add 15 cm for hems, i.e. 107 cm for each curtain. Multiply this by the number of panels required.

METHOD

1 Measure off the length for each panel and cut by the straight thread.

2 Turn down the depth of the hem on to the wrong side and press.

3 Turn down the depth of the hem again and tack (this double hem is to prevent the ragged edge of the net showing when the curtain is hung against the light). Machine along the edge of the hem. If the material is of a very open pattern, place tissue paper underneath when machining; this can be torn off afterwards.

4 Put another row of machining the depth of the rod plus 5 mm from the first row of machining, thus forming a slot (Fig. 36a).

The bottom hem may be tacked and stitched temporarily until after the curtains are washed, and when they have shrunk the hem may be let down and the permanent hems made and machined.

FESTOON STYLE (Fig. 35d) (Using curtain track)

This style of curtain covers the whole of the window and is made of very transparent plain fabrics.

Measure the depth of the window and allow half as much again for the drawing-up, plus the frills at the bottom. The width of the curtain depends upon the availability of the fabric, which is obtainable up to 3.66 metres wide. If it is necessary to have any joins, arrange for these to be hidden by the tapes.

1 Allowing for a border of 25-75 mm at each side, mark out the position of the festoons, usually 25-30 cm apart. Mark with a crease down the centre of each festoon. Stitch narrow terylene tape over each crease, starting 50 mm from the top of the curtain (Fig. 35e). Knot the ends of cords at the lower edge of each festoon.

2   Turn down the top hem but make sure ends of the cord of each festoon are free and attach the terylene tape as in Fig. 35e. Secure the ends of cord at one end.

3   Make a frill for bottom of curtain, the depth required plus 25 mm for hems by 1½ times the width of curtain. Make narrow hems at the ends of the frill and on bottom edge. On the remaining long edge attach terylene tape as for curtain heading (on wrong side) and draw up cords until frill fits curtain. Turn lower edge of curtain on to right side (Fig. 35f) and cover with the tape of the frill and machine into position.

4   Draw up the cords of the festoons to correct depth, knot cords and cut off.

HEADINGS

Valance (plain frill)

CHOICE OF MATERIAL

Most materials except very thick cretonnes and linens are suitable.

CALCULATION OF MATERIAL

Allow 1½ times the width of the window. The depth of the frill is usually about one-ninth of the total length of the curtain, unless the curtain is very short.

METHOD

1   Cut out the necessary number of strips, matching the pattern or design of the fabric.

2   Join the strips together with plain seams.

3   At both ends of the strip turn in 15 mm hems on to the wrong side.

4   At the top edge turn 30 mm of the material on to the wrong side and tack. Place the Rufflette tape half over the raw edge of the frill. Machine on the top and lower edge of the Rufflette tape as in Fig. 36b.

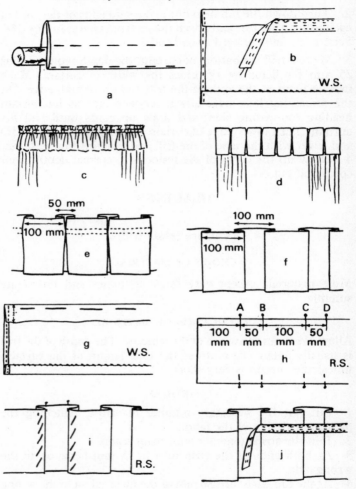

Figure 36

5 At the bottom of the frill turn a 30 mm hem on to the wrong side and slip hem.

6 Pull up the cords in the Rufflette tape so that the frill is equal to the width of the window (Fig. 36c).

Pleated frill

CHOICE OF MATERIAL

A good firm material is best, i.e. linen, velvet, etc. (Fig. 36d).

CALCULATION OF MATERIAL

If pleats are arranged as in Fig. 36e, allow 2½ times the width of the window, i.e. for a window 76 cm wide allow 190 cm of material. For pleats arranged as in Fig. 36f (note the space between the pleats) allow twice the width of the window space. The depth of the frill may be one-eighth to one-ninth of the total length of the curtain plus 80 mm for hems.

METHOD

Make as for valance (plain frill) diagrams (Method 1 to 3).

4 At the top edge turn down a 50 mm turning on to the wrong side and tack.

5 Turn up a 30 mm hem at the bottom on to the wrong side and slip hem (Fig. 36g).

6 Mark out the position for pleats by putting pins alternately 100 mm and 50 mm apart (Fig. 36h). The finished results of these pleats will look like Fig. 36f. Make the pleats by folding A over B. Make the rest of the pleats like these two (Fig. 36i). Press.

7 On the wrong side, attach Rufflette tape, after turning in the end. Lay Rufflette tape half over the raw edge of the pleated frill. Tack and machine along the top and lower edge of the Rufflette tape (Fig. 36j).

Note: For pleated material arranged in Fig. 36e place the pins 100 mm, 50 mm and 50 mm apart and repeat in this sequence the full length of the material. Make up as above.

Pinch pleats

CHOICE OF MATERIAL

A rich firm fabric such as velvet, taffeta, etc. is most suitable so that the pleats keep firmly in position. Make pinch-pleated heading as for curtains, using special tape and hooks.

Draperies

Draperies are a more formal type of finish for curtain headings (Fig. 37a). Always try out for size by first making up in muslin. There are two parts: a valance board covered by a draped valance; and cascades at each side. The draped valance should be the width of the board by about 76 cm deep (Fig. 37b). The lower edge should be curved and the sides should slope

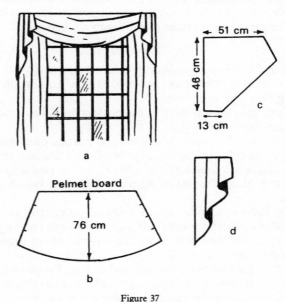

Figure 37

outwards at the bottom. Arrange in about four pleats at each side and pin to valance board. For the cascades cut out as in Fig. 37c, fold to form three pleats (Fig. 37d) and fit to valance board. The cascade usually turns the corner at the end of the board. To make up in curtain fabric, cut out material, using the muslin as a pattern. Make small hems all round or line the cascade. The edges may be finished off with a trimming.

PELMETS

DESIGNING OF PELMETS

The design of the pelmet should be in keeping with the architectural features of the room or window-frame. Many of the modern casement windows are very wide and therefore require narrow pelmets which are not elaborate in design (Fig. 38f, g). If the window is long and narrow as the Georgian windows or the Victorian sash window style, the pelmets should be deep and more elaborate in style and cut (Fig. 38a, b, c, d, and e). The depth of a pelmet is usually one-eighth to one-sixth of the height of the window. Shallow pelmets appear to give height to the room and are therefore used on modern windows. If the pelmet is deep (Fig. 38b) it is inclined to give the impression that the ceiling is lower.

SUITABLE MATERIALS

Heavy-weight fabrics such as velvet are suitable but light fabrics such as chintz may be used.

MEASUREMENTS

1 Measure the width of the window and add 150 mm on to this at both ends to allow for the portion of pelmet which goes round the pelmet rail or board at the sides (A to B of Fig. 39a).
2 The depth of the pelmet depends upon the size and shape of the window. Make a paper pattern and fit it to the pelmet rail so that you can decide upon the shape.

MATERIALS REQUIRED

1 The material should either match the curtains or tone in with them.

2 The lining should match the lining of the curtains.

3 Buckram. This is a heavy canvas which has been stiffened with size or glue. It is used to give shape to the pelmet. Tarpaulin can also be used as a substitute for buckram.

4 Braids may be used to decorate the pelmet.

5 A piece of Rufflette tape the length of the pelmet plus 30 mm is required to enable the pelmet to be attached to the rail.

CUTTING OUT

1 Mark out the pattern on to the buckram and cut out carefully (the buckram should not be joined, always cut out from the length).

2 Cut out the fabric with 30 mm turnings. If the material is not wide enough for the pelmet to be cut out in one piece, additional material should be added to both ends, and the pattern of the fabric should be matched at all seams.

3 The lining is cut out with 30 mm turnings.

MAKING THE PELMET

1 Tack the buckram on to the wrong side of the fabric, keeping it flat on a table. Coarse materials may be added to the buckram by pressing the two together, using a damp cloth on the fabric side and a hot iron.

2 Bring over the raw edge of the material on to the buckram and catch stitch. This is done by working from right to left; slip the needle along the fabric and then along the buckram (Fig. 39d).

3 Snip the turnings on curved and angular edges (Fig. 39b and c). Mitre the corners by folding the corner of the fabric over on to the buckram (Fig. 39e, stage 1). Fold down the top edge of the fabric on to the buckram (Fig. 39e, stage 2). Fold over the left-hand piece of fabric on to the buckram (Fig. 39e, stage 3), and slip hem the two folds together.

Figure 38

63

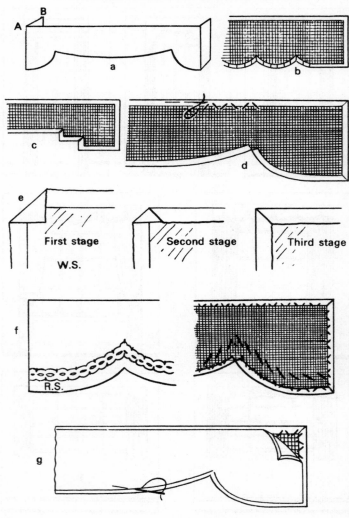

Figure 39 (a-g)

4 Any braid or fringe (Fig. 39i) should be put on at this stage. Use long stitches which are small on the right side but large on the wrong side (Fig. 39f).

5 Turn in the raw edge of the lining and hem on to the wrong side of the pelmet (Fig. 39g).

6 Place the Rufflette tape or heading tape 10-25 mm from the top of the pelmet and hem on the wrong side of the pelmet, making the ends firm and secure (Fig. 39h).

Note: If very fine fabrics are used, such as furnishing satin, an interlining may be placed between the fabric and buckram which will give a soft effect and prevent the coarse threads of the buckram making an impression on the right side of the fabric when pressed.

All pelmets should be dry-cleaned.

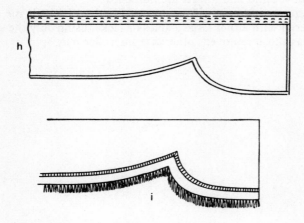

Figure 39 (h-i)

ROLLER BLINDS

These blinds are often required when a room is very sunny and the window large and there is need to keep the room cool in summer, or warm in winter. The blind may be used in a

65

kitchen, bathroom, etc. and also on doors with large areas of glass.

The blinds are simply made and kits are readily available from large stores. Specially treated fabric, available in several widths, may be purchased. Alternatively, tight, firmly woven fabrics, such as cottons, may be used, and treated with a stiffening agent.

RENOVATION

If the blind has become soiled or a change of decoration means a change of blind, then simply take the blind off the window fitting. Measure the amount of fabric required, plus the hem at the bottom. Make up by starting with the hem at the bottom; remove the lath from the old blind and insert into the hem of the new blind and attach the pull cord.

Remove old fabric from top of blind and attach the new material with either large staples or tacks, using only the same size as those removed, otherwise the roller may split.

CHAPTER 4

Loose covers for chairs, stools and dressing tables

Loose covers, or slip covers as they are often called, are essential aids in soft furnishing, as they enable us to hide an existing cover of a piece of furniture which does not fit into the colour scheme of a room. A loose cover may be used to protect the upholstered cover or to hide a shabby chair. The upholstery should be in a good condition before the cover is attempted as the latter cannot hide the shape of a badly worn chair. Covers can be made for nearly every type of chair but in a book of this size it is not possible to describe all of them. Three very different types of chairs have been chosen.

The most economical width of fabric is 77 cm. A 122 cm width is inclined to be wasteful. Odd pieces can be used for piping, frills, or for loose padded seats on dining-room chairs.

When fitting a loose cover stand at the back of the chair and place the back portion of the cover on first, the seat of the cover being away from you; work towards the front and fit each arm of the chair correctly; then tuck the cover well down into the seat of the chair. Smooth the cover all over and fasten up the placket and secure the underside of the chair. If the 'tuck in' of the cover is deep, insert a piece of rolled paper between the seat and the back in the 'tuck in'. This will prevent the cover from working up.

Loose cover for an upholstered chair

MEASUREMENTS FOR A CHAIR (make a note of all measurements)

1   Inside back: measure from A down the inside back of the

chair, across the seat and down to the lower edge to B, add 25 mm for each seam and 200 mm for 'tuck-in'. For the width, measure across the inside back of the chair, add 50 mm. This is usually the widest part, but check this with the front of seat measurements (Fig. 40a).

2 Outside back: measure A to C plus 50 mm (Fig. 40b).

3 Outside arm: measure D to E plus 50 mm. Multiply this measurement by two because of the two arms.

4 Inside arm: measure D to F plus 50 mm. Multiply this measurement by two because of the two arms.

5 Facing: measure G to H.

Note: 19.2 metres of crossway strips 30 mm wide can be cut from 1 metre of 77 cm width fabric.

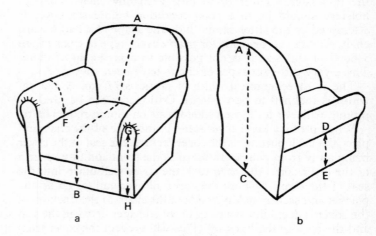

Figure 40

CUTTING OUT

First of all study the pattern of the fabric, note if it is reversible or not, and remember that flowers and trees must grow upwards; birds, animals and fruit must look in their natural positions.

1   Cut out the length of fabric for the inside back and seat. Pin to the back of the chair and to the lower edge of the seat. Tuck the material well in between inside back and seat. Arrange the fabric so that the main pattern motif is suitably placed.

Note: If the pattern of the fabric is bold, centre the design. This is done by placing the centre of the design in the centre back of the chair and the main design should repeat again on the seat.

2   The outside back piece may next be cut out and pinned in position.

3   The outside arm pieces should be cut alike and pinned to the chair. The pattern must be carefully matched.

4   The inside arm pieces must also be cut to match one another.

5   The facings must be cut so that they both have the same design of the fabric.

6   Leave half a metre for the flaps but do not cut off. This extra material is attached to the sides, back and front of the chair and goes underneath the bottom of the chair to prevent the loose cover from showing the upholstery.

Calculation of materials required

Corresponding to chair measurements	Section of chair	Widths of fabric required	Amount required with 'tuck in' cm	Total amount of 77 cm wide fabric cm
1	Inside back and seat	1	164	164
2	Outside back	1	74	74
3	Inside arm	2	71	142
4	Outside arm	2	46	92
5	Facings	1	51	51
6	Frills or flaps (Fig. 36)	1	71	71
7	Piping			

Total amount of 77 cm wide fabric = 6.0 metres

7 Cut out the crossway strips 40 mm wide and sufficient to be inserted in all the important seams. If in doubt look at the permanent upholstered cover and note where piping or cord is used.

Figure 41

MAKING OF COVER

1 Prepare the piping (Fig. 10).

2 Pin the piping along the front edge of the seat. Turn under the raw edge of the front band and pin to the piping (Fig. 42a). Join together with lock stitch (Fig. 42b).

3 Tack the inside and outside arm pieces together. A piping may be inserted in the seam.

4 Carefully arrange the fullness at the front of the arms into pleats. The same number of pleats must be on both arms.

5 Make a paper pattern of the exact shape of the front arm facings by pinning a piece of paper on to the chair and pencil-marking the shape of the facing on to it, and then cut out. Place the pattern on to the right side of the material previously cut out for the facing and tack round it (Fig. 42c). Tack the piping round the edge of the facing (Fig. 42d).

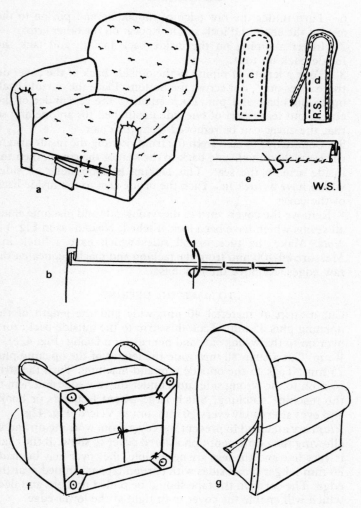

Figure 42

71

6   Turn under the raw edge of the facing and pin on to the arm of the chair and lock stitch. Repeat on the other arm.

7   Insert a piping on the inside back facing, and tack the inside back on to it.

8   Tack a length of piping to the outside back of the cover on three sides only, not across the bottom. Place the outside back on to the chair and pin. Lock stitch to the remainder of the cover, but leave part of one side unstitched for an opening so that the cover can be removed from the chair.

9   Commence to tack from the front, joining the inside arm to the seat; then the inside back to the seat of the cover; then the inside arm to the seat. This tacking is done along all sides which have a 'tuck in'. Tack the inside arm to the inside back of the cover.

Remove the cover, turn to the wrong side and machine along all seams which have been lock stitched. Neaten, as in Fig. 14. *Note:* Make the tuck on all sides which have a 'tuck in'. Measure 80-100 mm from the tacking and machine, neaten the raw edges. Remove the tackings.

TO MAKE THE OPENING

Cut a strip of material 40 mm wide and the length of the opening plus 25 mm. Tack this strip to the outside back, turn over on to the wrong side and hem as for a facing (Fig. 42e).

Wrap. Cut a strip 80 mm wide the length of the opening plus 25 mm. Tack to the outside arm and machine. Turn the strip over on to the wrong side, turn under the raw edge and hem to the machine stitching. Stitch large patent fasteners or hooks and eyes alternately every 50 mm, or use Velcro (Fig. 42g).

Flaps are attached to prevent the cover from working up and so allowing the permanent upholstered cover to show. If the chair is very low and the legs are not visible, the cover may be made 80 mm longer on all sides with curtain tape machined near the edge. The cords in the tape should be pulled up tight and tied, which will enable the cover to fit tight at the lower edge.

The flaps should be 130 mm deep and the length should be equal to the sides of the chair minus the width of the legs. Hem the flaps on three sides and attach to the cover. Stitch on tapes, which tie underneath the chair (Fig. 42f).

Loose cover for occasional chair

Covers can be made for chairs with wooden arms, but these covers must have two back openings.

CUTTING OUT

1   Cut out a length of fabric for the inside back and seat. This should equal A to B plus 100 mm for tuck in and 50 mm for turnings. The width should be the inside back of the chair plus 50 mm (C to D, Fig. 43a).

2   The outside back is next cut out, the size being A to B plus 150 mm and C to D plus 50 mm (Fig. 43b).

3   Front of seat. The depth of the strip is B to F plus 150 mm and wide enough to reach from one arm round the front of the seat to the next arm (Fig. 43c).

4   Side bands. Measure from the arm to the back of the chair plus 50 mm, the depth being equal to G to H plus 150 mm.

5   Cut out crossway strips 40 mm wide and sufficient to go round the seat and the back of the chair. Measure from the back leg up the side, across the top and down the next side to the other leg.

MAKING UP

1   Prepare the piping (Fig. 10).

2   On the inside back of the cover fold back the material level with the wood of the arm (Fig. 43d). Cut across the material from A to within 25 mm of the arm at B. Snip the material from B to the corners of the wooden arm (Fig. 43e).

3   Fold back the turnings which have been cut (Fig. 43f). Bring the lower piece of fabric under the arm towards the outside back of the chair. Bring the upper piece of the folded fabric over the arm and towards the outside back of the chair and pin. Repeat this for the other arm.

73

Remove this part of the cover and face the parts which have been cut. This is done by the following method:

(a) Place the inside back of the chair cover flat on to a table, wrong side uppermost.

(b) Place a piece of material 150 mm square underneath the cut part (Fig. 43g). Machine along the crease marks as in Fig. 43g).

(c) Cut the material away to within 12 mm of the machine stitching and snip into the corners, as in Fig. 43h.

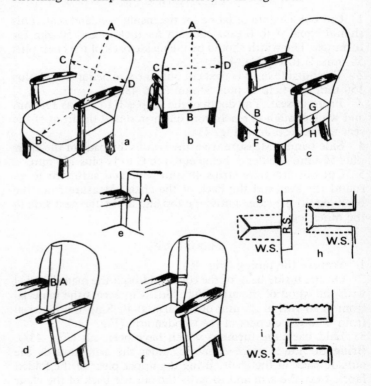

Figure 43 (a-i)

74

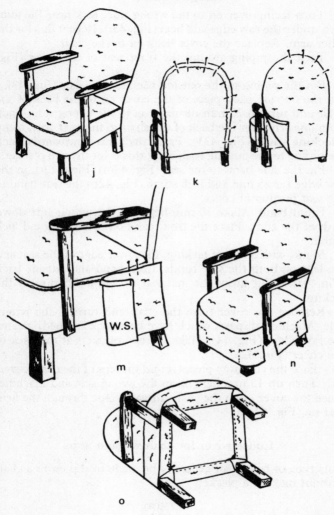

Figure 43 (j-o)

(d) Turn facing over on to the wrong side, tack near the join, turn under the raw edge and hem (Fig. 43i). Repeat this for the other arm. Replace the cover back on to the chair.

4 Tack the piping around the front seat of the cover (Fig. 43j).

5 Pin the piping to the outside back of the chair (Fig. 43k). Pin the outside back piece of the cover on to the back of the chair and turn in 25 mm turnings on to the wrong side. Tack from one arm over the back of the chair to the next arm, using a locking stitch (Fig. 43l). From the arms downwards, tack the piping to the outside back only; this is for the two plackets.

6 Pin the side band to the seat (Fig. 43m). First, turn in the raw edge for 25 mm and lock stitch (Fig. 42b) the side band to the seat portion of cover.

7 Front band. Make 10 mm hems on the wrong side down both of the ends. Place the front band on to the seat and lock stitch.

8 Mark, with a row of tacking, the lower edge of the seat and the legs on both the side bands, front band and outside back (Fig. 43n). Cut away the material to within 15 mm of the tacking.

9 Remove the cover from the chair and turn to the wrong side. Machine all parts which have been lock stitched. Neaten the raw edges (Fig. 14). Make the two plackets at the back of the cover (Fig. 42e).

10 Face the cut-away pieces round the legs of the chair cover.

11 Turn up 15 mm hem on to the wrong side and machine. Place the cover on to the chair, thread a tape through the hem and tie (Fig. 43o).

Loose cover for chair without arms

This type of cover can generally be made to slip on to a chair without making a placket.

METHOD

1 Cut out a length of fabric for the inside back and seat. This

should equal A to B plus 100 mm for tuck in and 50 mm for turnings. The width should be the inside back of the chair plus 50 mm, C to D (Fig. 44a).

2   The outside back is then cut out. The size should be A to E plus 50 mm and C to D plus 50 mm (Fig. 44b).

3   Side band. Cut out a strip of material equal in depth to B to F plus 50 mm and long enough to go round the front of the chair from G to H plus 50 mm (Fig. 44c).

4   Frill. Measure from G to H round the front of the seat, plus the width of the back of the chair. 200 mm must be added on for each pleat. The pleats may be at the front legs of the chair and not at the back. The depth of the frill should be measured from the lower edge of the seat, F, to the floor, I. Add 50 mm for hems (Fig. 44c).

5   Place the inside back and seat on to the chair, tuck the material into the space between the inside back and the seat for 100 mm (Fig. 44d). Pin the cover into position.

6   Turn in the raw edge of the side band for 25 mm, then pin it to the seat. Lock stitch (Fig. 42b) the side band to the seat portion of the cover (Fig. 44e).

7   Pin the outside back piece of the cover to the back of the chair and turn in 25 mm turnings on to the wrong side. Lock stitch to the front of the cover (Fig. 44f).

8 (a)   Turn under the top edge of the frill for 25 mm (Fig. 44g), then pin the frill to the side band.

8 (b)   Make a 200 mm inverted pleat at the corner of the seat. This is done by placing a pin at the top edge of the frill at the join of the leg to the seat. This is pin No. 1 (Fig. 44h). Measure 100 mm to pin No. 2 and another 100 mm to pin No. 3 (Fig. 44i). Fold the material over so that pin No. 1 meets pin No. 2 (Fig. 44j). Then fold the material so that pin No. 3 meets pin No. 2. Tack along the pleat to make it secure. Continue to pin the frill on to the chair and make another inverted pleat at the next join of leg to the seat. Continue to pin the frill on to the seat all round (Fig. 44k). Tack the frill on to the cover with lock stitch (Fig. 42b).

9   Remove the cover and machine together on the tack line on

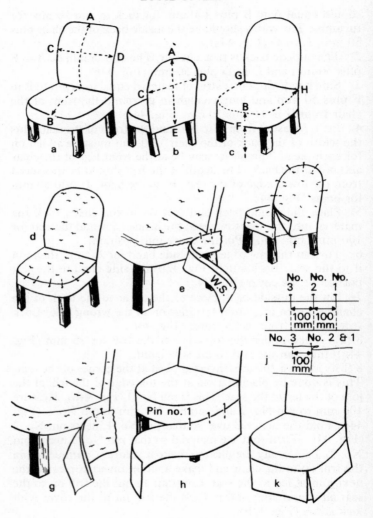

Figure 44

78

the wrong side. Neaten the raw edge (Fig. 13c). A cord may be stitched on to the right side of the cover. The cord should be placed over the seams and stitched as on Fig. 11.

Frills for chair covers

Frills may be used for two purposes: either for a decorative finish in keeping with a valance used for the curtain heading, or to hide badly disfigured legs of a chair. The frill may have the fullness arranged in different ways.

DEPTH OF FRILLS

A frill should reach to within 10 mm of the floor. The depth is measured from the lower edge of the cover to the floor plus 40 mm, allowing for a 15 mm seam at the top and a 25 mm hem at the lower edge.

GATHERED FRILLS

1   For a gathered frill measure round the chair and add on half as much again, i.e. for a chair measuring 230 cm add 115 cm = 345 cm. Several widths of fabric would be required, e.g. if the width of fabric was 77 cm, divide 345 cm by 77 cm = 4½ widths. Each width should be cut to the depth required.

2   Join the widths together to form a continuous length, and make a 25 mm hem at the bottom of the frill. Place in a gathering thread (gathering stitch, Fig. 3) 15 mm from the top edge of the frill, draw up the gathering thread so that the frill fits the cover and secure the thread.

3   Place the right side of the frill to the right side of the cover, space out the gathers evenly, tack, machine and neaten.

Note: In some styles of chairs the front legs are higher than the back, thus giving a side view appearance of the chair seat sloping towards the rear. The frill, when attached, should be at the same level all the way round as at the front of the chair, therefore a row of pins should be placed in the cover, marking the depth of the front edge of the cover from the floor all round.

PLEATED FRILL

1 For a pleated frill, measure all round the chair and add three-quarters of the measurement for the pleats, i.e. if the measurement round the chair is 204 cm, three-quarters of it is 153 cm, giving a total of 357 cm. This is the length of the strip required for pleating.

2 Cut out the necessary number of widths, matching the pattern. The depth should be equal to the finished depth of the frill plus 40 mm. Join the widths together as in Fig. 12.

3 Turn up 25, mm hem on the lower edge of the frill and either slip hem or machine.

4 Mark out the position of the pleats by placing a pin near the beginning of the fabric. This is pin No. 1. Measure 60 mm to pin No. 2. From this pin measure 100 mm to pin No. 3. From here measure 60 mm to pin No. 4. Continue placing pins 100 mm and 60 mm alternately (Fig. 45a).

5 Pin the pleats into position by folding the material so that pin No. 1 touches No. 2. No. 4 pin meets No. 3 (Fig. 45b and c). Continue folding the pleats first one way then the other. Tack and press. Attach to the chair as in Point 3 of gathered frill.

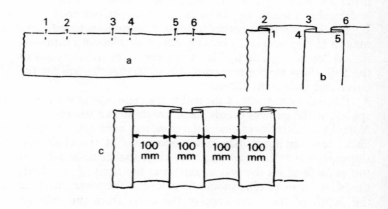

Figure 45

PLEATED FRILL FOR AN OCCASIONAL CHAIR

When a frill is required for a chair with wooden arms, the frill has to be made detachable along the sides of the chair.

The chair cover should reach the lower edge of the seat. The frill should be made up as for pleated frill (Fig. 45a), and the piping stitched to the upper edge of the frill. The frill is pinned along the front edge of the chair and stitched. The portion of the frill which extends across the side of the chair should be faced at the upper edge and attached to the seat portion of the cover by means of press studs. A separate frill is attached to the back of the chair cover.

Arm caps

These are small detachable caps used on the arms of chairs to protect the covers and are easily laundered. The caps are made to fit the arms of the chair and can be cut from any odd piece of material left over from making the loose covers.

Figure 46

For moquette suites, a coarse cotton can be used for the crochet of arm pieces; chair-backs can also be made to match (Fig. 46).

Settee cover

The idea of covering a settee may seem at first to present alarming difficulties. This should not be so, as the processes involved are similar to those of an upholstered chair (pp. 67–73). The only difference is that the back and seat are wider, therefore the width of the fabric will not be sufficient for the breadth of the back and seat. In this case the joins must be equally spaced at both sides. Great care must be taken to ensure the complete matching of the additional material in order to give a unified appearance.

Loose chair cover (small size)

MATERIALS REQUIRED

1.6 metres of 77 cm wide material.
1 hank of medium piping cord.
1 reel of cotton to match.
1 card of patent fasteners.

PREPARATION

1   Make a paper pattern the exact shape and size of the chair seat (Fig. 47).
2   If chair is small and pattern on material large, arrange to have the main pattern in the centre of the seat.
3   Selvedge threads run from front to back of the chair seat and from the upper edge to lower one of the side bands and frills.
4   Flowers must grow in the proper direction, i.e. from front to back.
5   If material is very thick choose a thin piping cord and prepare the piping as in Fig. 10.

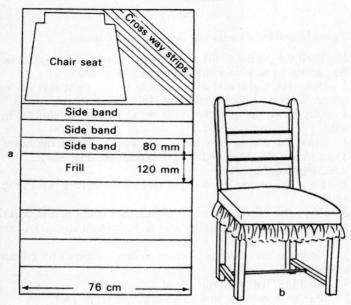

Figure 47

CUTTING OUT

1 Lay the paper pattern on to the material, pin and cut out, allowing 15 mm turnings.

2 Cut side bands the depth required (80-100 mm) and sufficient to go round the chair plus 300 mm for the back plackets.

3 Cut frill the desired depth (120 mm) by weft thread. For a gathered frill allow 1½ times the circumference of the chair, and for a pleated frill twice the circumference.

4 Cut the crossway strips 40 mm wide and sufficient to go round the chair.

5 If there is to be no frill, cut a false hem 50 mm in depth, weft way.

83

METHOD

To make the faced corners at the back of the seat

1 Tack the piping to the corner of the cover on the right side. Be careful to tack to a straight thread (Fig. 48a).

2 Place the right side of the facing to the right side of the cover. Tack and backstitch (Fig. 48b).

3 Snip down the material at the corners to the stitching (Fig. 48b).

4 Turn the facing over on to the wrong side of the cover. Turn in the raw edge and hem into position (Fig. 48c).

Attaching band to seat

1 Tack the piping to the right side of the border piece (Fig. 48d).

2 Place the border 90 mm beyond the corner of the cover, with the right sides together and tack through all thicknesses (Fig. 48e).

3 Tack the back border piece on so that it extends for 60 mm at both ends.

4 Machine, using a piping foot.

5 Blanket stitch the raw edges together (Fig. 13c).

Finishing the lower edge of cover

A false hem may be used as in Fig. 48f, or a pleated or gathered frill may also be used to finish the lower edge of the cover. To make the frill:

1 Join up the widths, turn in a narrow hem and machine.

2 Pleat or gather, using attachment on the machine.

3 Place right side of frill to the right side of border and machine close to the piping cord.

4 Neaten the raw edges by machine or blanket stitch.

Placket or opening

1 Fit the cover on to the chair and mark the fitting line. The side band of the chair cover goes under the back band.

2 Remove the piping cord to the edge of the fitting line.

3 Turn in the raw edges and make a hem about 20 mm in depth.

4 Stitch on the patent fasteners or use Velcro.

84

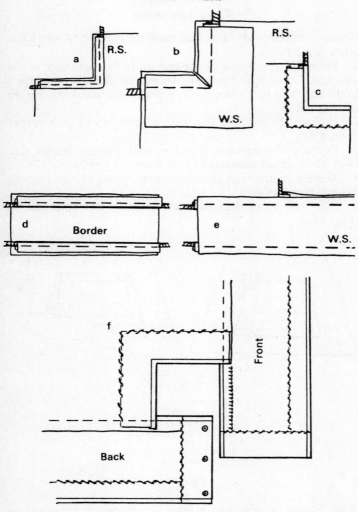

Figure 48

Chair seat cover

Chairs with removable seats can easily be covered to match the other furnishings.

1 Place the upper side of the seat on to the right side of the material. Cut out, allowing 80-100 mm on all sides (Fig. 49a). Make sure that the centre motif of design is in the centre before cutting out.

2 Pull up the sides of the material and pin at each corner (Fig. 49b).

3 Remove the seat and machine down the pin marks. Cut away the surplus material 15 mm from the stitching.

4 Make a 15 mm hem all round on the wrong side and thread narrow tape through the hem.

5 Place the cover over the seat, draw up the tapes and tie (Fig. 49c).

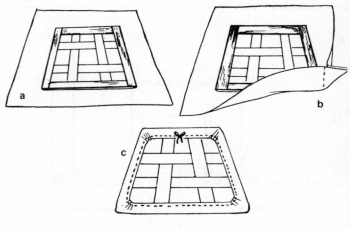

Figure 49

Note: Elastic may be used in place of tape or curtain draw tape stitched on, and the cords in the tape drawn up.

Loose cover for stool

A stool may have a loose cover which can easily be removed and laundered and which should harmonize with the general colour scheme of the room.

CUTTING OUT

1   Cut out a piece of material with the chief motif of the design in the centre of the cover. The length must be equal to the length of the stool, plus twice the depth of the upholstery, plus 50 mm for turnings. The width is equal to the width of the stool plus twice the depth of the upholstery, plus 50 mm.

2   Cut sufficient crossway strips to go round the stool once.

3   Cut two strips 80 mm wide and the length of the stool minus 25 mm. Cut two strips 80 mm wide to fit the width of the stool minus 25 mm. (These pieces are used for flaps for the underside of the stool.)

METHOD

Prepare the piping as in Fig. 10.

1   Place the material, right side uppermost, on to the stool, pin the corners as in Fig. 50a, and slip tack (large slip hemming).

2   Pin the piping cord to the lower edge of the stool (Fig. 50b) and tack. (Join the crossway strips of the piping, and the piping cord as in Fig. 10.)

3   Turn in a hem on three sides of the flaps and machine.

4   Place the side flaps to the sides of the stool, turn under the raw edge of the flaps, pin to the piping (Fig. 50c) and tack.

5   Remove the cover. Turn to the wrong side, machine down the tacking at each corner, trim the surplus material to within 15 mm of the machining (Fig. 50d) and neaten the raw edge by blanket stitch. Machine the flaps and the piping on to the cover and neaten the raw edges.

6   Replace the cover on to the stool. Turn the stool over (Fig. 50e) and fasten the corners of the flaps to each other by stitching on hooks and eyes (Fig. 50f) or stitch on strips of Velcro, but the strips must overlap to fasten.

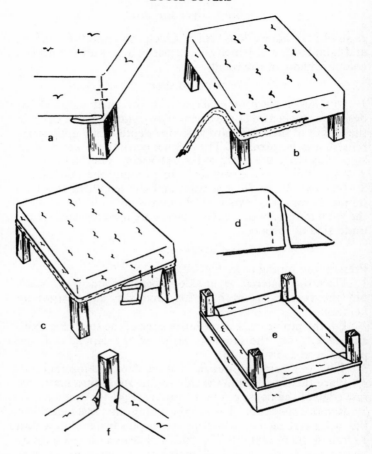

Figure 50

Ideas for stools

In most bedrooms there is a stool. It may be oblong as in Fig. 50, or it may be a piano stool (Fig. 51a), which could be covered with a complete circle of material with a scalloped edge which could either be faced or bound. A cord tied round 40 mm below the top edge of the stool gives the scallops a fluted effect (Fig. 51d). The frill is a straight piece of fabric gathered.

The top of the stool may be embroidered and the side band finely pleated, also the frill. According to the prevailing fashions of textiles, the frill could be permanently pleated (Fig. 51e).

The stool with a round top (Fig. 51b) may have a cover made like the pouffe (Fig. 52a).

A box could also be used as a stool (Fig. 51c), and the top may have a pad of foam and can be covered like a day divan, page 105.

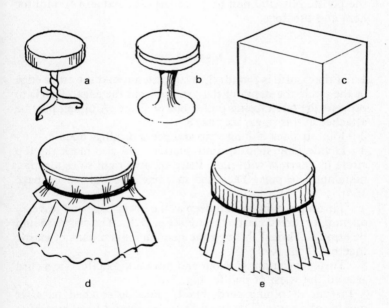

Figure 51

Pouffe cover

Covers for a pouffe can be quickly made and extra material could be purchased when making loose covers for chairs, curtains, or cushions so that the pouffe fits into the colour scheme of a room.

1   One piece of fabric the size of the top of the pouffe and 25 mm for turnings.

2   A strip of fabric to go round the pouffe (not too tightly) and 25 mm turnings. The depth of fabric should be the depth of the pouffe plus 100 mm to go underneath and also 50 mm for hem and turnings.

1   If the pouffe is round, then run stitch round the outer edge of the circle the depth of the turning from the edge. This is to prevent the circle being pulled out of shape. A piping may be attached at this stage, see page 8.

2   Join up sides of long strip and press turnings open.

3   Divide long strip up into quarters and also mark the top circle in quarters with pins. Place the two right sides together matching the pins. Tack and machine (see Fig. 93 on page 164).

4   Turn up a hem 15 mm deep at the lower edge and leave an opening to thread elastic through (Fig. 52b). The elastic should be strong. Thread through the hem and stitch ends of elastic together (Fig. 52c).

5   Turn cover right side out and put on to pouffe. Tie a cord around the waist of pouffe (Fig. 52a).

Instead of piping cord, braid could be stitched on after making the cover. The braid and cord should be of matching design and colour.

90

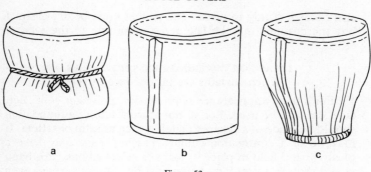

a   b   c

Figure 52

Dressing tables

According to periods of fashion and taste, dressing tables have been covered with drapes. The most popular design is kidney-shaped. Basically the dressing table can be a chest of drawers or two smaller sets of drawers with a top piece of wood which extends beyond the chest, thus enabling a curtain rail to be attached to the underside of the wood. The curtains need only go round three sides of the table. To enable easy access to the drawers the curtains should be in two sections and should meet at the front.

Make up as for unlined curtains (Fig. 33, page 49) but place the heading tape 5-10 mm from the top edge of the curtain.

PELMET AND TOP OF DRESSING TABLE

Cut a piece of material the size of the top, plus 25 mm all round. The pelmet can go all round the table with a join at the back. A piece of buckram should be cut out to the desired design; this may be straight or shaped. Make up as Fig. 39, page 64, but do not turn down the top edge. Mark the centre front and back of the top cover and pelmet. Pin carefully, then join. Line the pelmet.

Place on to the dressing table and cover with sheet glass cut to the shape of the table. This protects the fabric from dirt and also holds it firmly in place. The pelmet must be dry-cleaned but the curtains may be laundered according to the type of fabric.

IDEAS FOR COVERING DRESSING TABLES
(When curtains are purely decorative)

1   For a dainty appearance swiss muslin, polyester voile, net, lace, etc. can be used. For all transparent fabrics a foundation should be made of a cheaper material such as satin or taffeta. It may be of a contrasting colour. The top edge may have a pleated band held in place by satin or velvet ribbon (this band would require a firm foundation of stiffer fabric, perhaps even bonded material) (Fig. 53a).

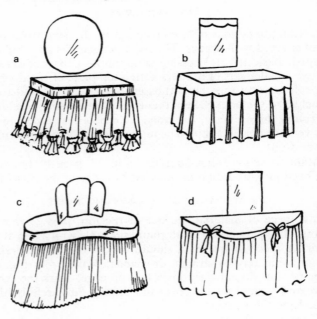

Figure 53

2   For a more tailored effect a shaped pelmet could be used with groups of pleats arranged at each scallop. (Ask your fabric store for advice about the fabric for this design.) The top of the mirror may be decorated with a matching border (Fig. 53b).

3   A quilted chintz pelmet could be used with a permanently knife-pleated curtain. This would depend upon trends in textiles (Fig. 53c).

4   Instead of using a covered buckram pelmet, try a broad sash. This would really be a soft piece of fabric attached like a pelmet but without any stiffening. Broad bows could be added for decoration (Fig. 53d).

Loose cover for a head-board

A loose cover may be made for the head-board of a bed, either to match the bed-cover or to contrast with it.

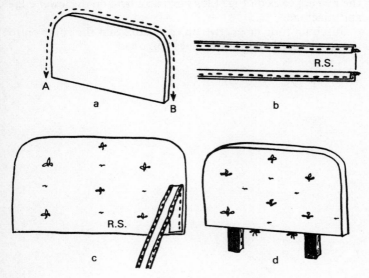

Figure 54

CUTTING OUT

1   Cut two pieces the shape of the head-board plus 25 mm.
2   Cut a strip long enough to go round the head-board from A to B (Fig. 54a). The width should be equal to the thickness of the head-board plus 25 mm.
Note: If the wood is very thin, this strip may be omitted and the two pieces of material joined together with a piping cord.
3   Cut crossway strips, twice the length of the strip.

METHOD

1   Prepare the piping as in Fig. 10.
2   Tack the piping on to both edges of the side band on the right side (Fig. 54b).
3   Pin the right side of the side band to the right side of the front panel and tack (Fig. 54c). Machine, using a piping foot. Tack the back panel on in the same way and machine. Neaten the raw edges as on Fig. 13c. Turn up a hem on the lower edge and machine.

Stitch on four tapes, two on each side. Slip the cover on to the head-board and tie the tapes (Fig. 54d).

CHAPTER 5

Bed-covers, duvets and eiderdowns

There are three main types of bed for which covers are made. First, the bed with panelled head and foot. The cover for this has a frill on two sides only. Second, the bedstead with an open framework at the head and foot. This has a cover with a frill on each side and a detached frill at the foot, which is slipped between the mattress and the bedstead. The third is the divan bed, the cover for which has a frill on each side and one at the foot. If the divan is in a bed-sitting room its cover may have a frill all round (Fig. 60a and b).

The sizes of beds vary considerably and the size of the cover depends upon the width of the bed and the length, also the height from the ground when the bed is made. From these measurements one can calculate the amount of fabric necessary for making the cover.

When duvets are used, the cover for the duvet is made to match or link up with the colours of the sheet and valance. A bedspread would be used to cover the whole of the bed and the fabric could tone with that of the curtains. Bed-covers are often made of the same fabric as the curtains or loose chair-cover, and therefore are either made of fabric which can be dry-cleaned, or laundered.

Making a single bedspread

SIZE OF BED

Approximately 90 cm by 200 cm and 56 cm high (top of the bed-clothes to the ground).

CHOICE OF MATERIAL

A medium-weight fabric which does not crease easily.

AMOUNT OF MATERIAL REQUIRED

5.5 metres of 122 cm wide fabric.

CUTTING OUT

1   From the length of material cut one piece 2.75 metres long by 94 mm wide.
2   Divide the remaining 2.75 metres into two pieces, each being 2.75 metres by 61 mm wide (Fig. 55a).

METHOD

1   Join the 61 mm wide pieces of fabric to each side of the 94 mm wide piece, matching the pattern if possible. The seam used should be a plain one, neatened on the wrong side.
2   Make a 25 mm hem down each side and a 50 mm hem at the top and bottom.
Note: If a reversible patterned fabric is used (i.e. one which has a pattern printed equally on both sides so that it can be reversed), join the widths together using a run and fell seam. Cover the seam on both sides by using a braid 10 to 12 mm wide. Make a 25 mm hem down each side and cover the stitches of the hem with braid. Turn under a 50 mm hem at the top and bottom of the cover and again use braid to give a finish to the cover (Fig. 55b).

When making a bedspread never have a join down the centre of the cover. Seams must always be placed at equal distances from the centre panel (Fig. 55b).

This type of bed-cover may have the corners at the foot rounded and a deep fringed braid used as an edging.

Making a cover for a double bed

SIZE OF BED

Approximately 135 cm by 200 cm and 61 cm high.

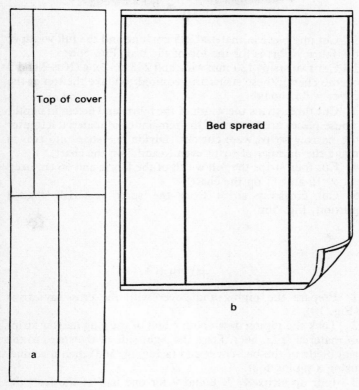

Figure 55

CHOICE OF MATERIALS

Most of the medium weight fabrics are suitable, but preference should be given to a material which does not crease easily.

AMOUNT OF MATERIAL REQUIRED

7.6 metres, 122 cm wide (plain or small pattern). 9.8 metres piping cord (medium).

97

CUTTING OUT

1   Cut one piece of material 245 cm long and the full width of the fabric. This is for the top of the bed (Fig. 56b).

2   Cut two strips 130 mm wide and 245 cm long (Nos 2 and 3 on the chart); these strips are required to make the top of the cover wide enough.

3   Cut three strips the width of the fabric and 66 cm in depth. These pieces are cut out of the remainder of material left after the narrow strips were cut out. Divide one strip into two to make the number of strips even (6 and 7 on the chart).

4   Cut four strips the full width of the fabric and 66 cm deep (8, 9, 10 and 11 on the chart).

5   Cut crossway strips from the spare material (shaded portion, Fig. 56b).

METHOD

1   Prepare the piping and cover with the crossway strips (Fig. 10).

2   Tack the piping down both edges of the long narrow strips of material (Fig. 56c). Place the right side of the strips to the right side of the bed-cover and tack (Fig. 56d) then machine, using a piping foot.

3   Join up strips 4, 7, 8 and 9 for one half of the frill, the remainder are for the other half.

4   Alter the stitch on the machine to a larger size, for gathering. Machine 20 mm from the top on both pieces. Draw up the frill to the required size (230 cm) by pulling one of the threads in the machine stitching.

5   Place the flounce or frill 150 mm from the bottom of the bed-cover with the two right sides together; tack through all the thicknesses (Fig. 56e). Machine, using a piping foot.

6   Neaten all the raw edges. Face the 150 mm strip on the foot of the cover (Fig. 56f).

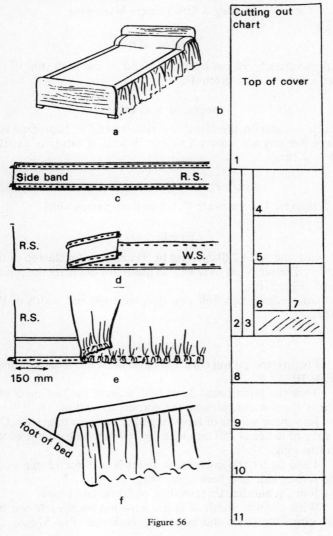

Figure 56

99

Making a fitted single bed-cover

SIZE OF BED

Approximately 90 cm by 190 cm and 51 cm high (top of the bed-clothes to the ground).

CHOICE OF MATERIALS

Small designs on the fabric are more restful in bedrooms and large designs are wasteful to cut. Width of fabric is usually 76-122 cm.

AMOUNT OF MATERIAL REQUIRED

6.2 metres, 122 cm wide. 5.5 metres of piping cord.

CUTTING OUT

1   Cut one piece 220 cm long by 94 cm wide for the top of the cover. The strip left over will be useful for covering the piping cord (Fig. 57b).
2   Cut seven strips 560 mm deep and the full width of the fabric.

METHOD

1   Prepare the piping cord and cover with the crossway strips (Fig. 10).
2   Tack the piping cord down both sides of the bed-cover and across the bottom, turning the corners as on Fig. 10.
3   Join three widths of fabric together on the wrong side. Cut a strip of material 250 mm wide by 560 mm long off one of the widths (Fig. 57c).
4   Turn under the raw edge at point A to B for 12 mm on to the wrong side and hem (Fig. 57d).
5   Join up another three widths of fabric and repeat.
6   With the one width of fabric left, join on to each end the 250 mm wide strips and hem down each side (Fig. 57e).

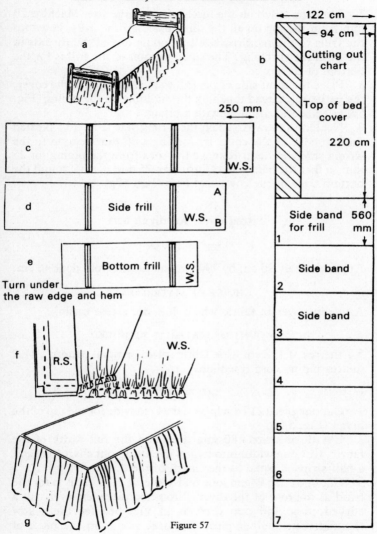

Figure 57

101

7 Alter the stitch on the machine to a large size. Machine 20 mm from the top on all the three pieces of the frills. Draw up the frills to the required size by pulling one of the threads in the machine stitching. The small portion of the frill is for the bottom of the cover.

8 Place the right side of the frill to the right side of the cover, the gathering thread touching the stitching on the piping (Fig. 57f). Tack and machine with a piping foot.

9 Neaten the raw edges on the wrong side (Fig. 13). Neaten the top edge of the cover by turning a 25 mm hem on to the wrong side and hem. Remove the cord from the piping for 25 mm so that the hem is flat. Turn up a 25 mm hem all round the bottom edge of the cover and hem (Fig. 57g).

Fitted cover for divan bed

SIZE OF DIVAN

Approximately 90 cm by 190 cm and height from floor 46 cm.

CHOICE OF MATERIALS

A medium weight fabric which does not crease easily.

AMOUNT OF MATERIAL REQUIRED

5.7 metres of 122 cm wide fabric (plain or small pattern). 11.1 metres piping cord (medium).

CUTTING OUT

1 Cut one piece 215 cm long and 94 cm wide for the top of the divan (Fig. 58a).

2 Cut three strips 180 mm deep and the full width of the fabric. Cut one width into two as in cutting-out chart (one and a half strips is equal to the length of the divan).

3 Cut one strip 94 cm long and 180 mm deep. This is for the band at the foot of the divan. From the piece left over, cut a curved piece 140 mm deep as in Fig. 58a for the pillow shaping. Cut another piece the same size from the piece of

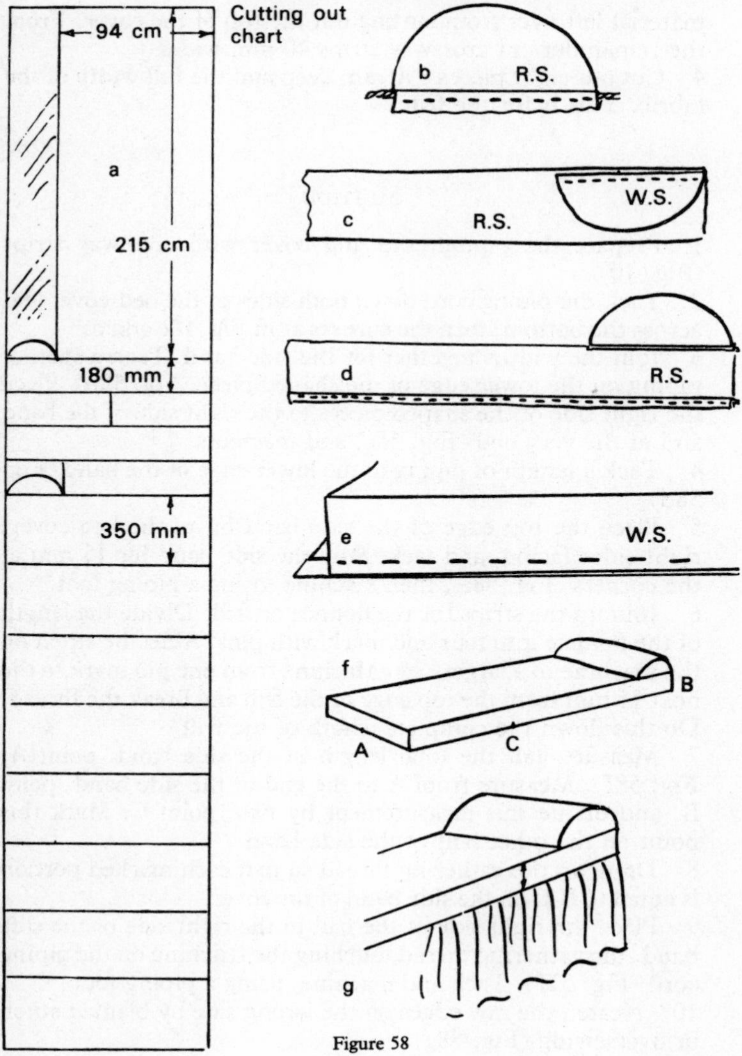

Cutting out
chart

Figure 58

103

material left over from cutting out the top of the cover. From the remainder cut crossway strips 40 mm wide.

4   Cut out eight pieces 350 mm deep and the full width of the fabric. This is for the frill.

METHOD

1   Prepare the piping cord and cover with crossway strips (Fig. 10).

2   Tack the piping cord down both sides of the bed-cover and across the bottom; turn the corners as in Fig. 10c and d.

3   Join the widths together for the side band. Tack a strip of piping on the lower edge of the shaped piece (Fig. 58b). Place the right side of the shaped pieces to the right side of the band and at the very end (Fig. 58c) and machine.

4   Tack a length of piping to the lower edge of the band (Fig. 58d).

5   Place the top edge of the side band on to the bed-cover, right sides facing, and tack. Snip the side band for 15 mm at the corners (Fig. 58e), then machine, using a piping foot.

6   Join up the strips for the flounce or frill. Divide the length of the flounce into four and mark with pins. Alter the stitch on the machine to a larger size. Machine from one pin mark to the next 15 mm from the top edge of the frill and break the thread. Do this down the complete length of the frill.

7   Measure half the total length of the side band, point A, Fig. 58f). Measure from A to the end of the side band, point B, and divide this measurement by two, point C. Mark this point on the other half of the side band.

8   Draw up the gathering thread so that each marked portion is equal to B-C on the side band of the cover.

9   Place the right side of the frill to the right side of the side band, the gathering thread touching the stitching on the piping cord (Fig. 57f). Tack and machine, using a piping foot.

10   Neaten the raw edges on the wrong side by blanket stitch or oversewing (Fig. 58g).

Day cover for divan

SIZE OF BED

Approximately 90 cm by 200 cm and 54 cm high.

CHOICE OF MATERIALS

A material which is fairly crease-resistant is essential and the thickness of the fabric depends upon the style required. A linen is best for pleated frills because it is firm and the pleats stay in position.

AMOUNT OF MATERIAL REQUIRED

Decide upon the type of pleated frill required and for full pleats allow three times the total measurement round the bed. It is best to take several strips of paper and pleat it to the desired design, so that it fits round the bed, and then calculate the amount of fabric required.

The example given is for very small folds of fabric to form pleats.

7.4 metres of 122cm wide (plain fabric).

12 metres piping cord.

CUTTING OUT

1   Cut out a piece of material for the top of the divan, the length being equal to the length of divan plus 40 mm, and the width of the material equal to the width of divan plus 40 mm (the strip that is left will be used for crossway strips) (Fig. 59b).

2   Cut five pieces the depth of the side band (180 mm) plus 40 mm for turnings = 220 mm and the full width of the fabric.

3   The depth of the frill is equal to B to C (360 mm) plus 70 mm for hem and turnings = 430 mm. Cut ten strips 430 mm deep and the full width of the fabric. (This is sufficient to go round all four sides of the divan.)

Cutting out chart

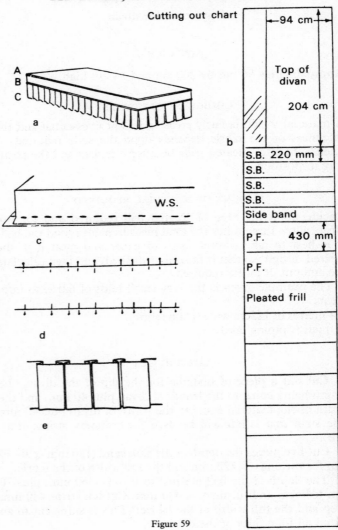

Figure 59

106

METHOD

1 Prepare the piping cord and cover with crossway strips (Fig. 10).

2 Place the piping to the edge of the cover and turn the corners as in Fig. 10c and d.

3 Join the strips of the side band and press the seams open. Place the right side of the side band to the right side of the cover and tack 20 mm from the edge. Snip the side band at the corners for 20 mm (Fig. 59c). Machine, using piping foot.

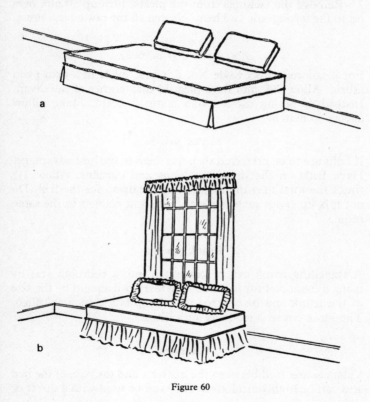

Figure 60

4   Tack the raw edge of the piping to the lower edge of the band.

5   Mark out the position of the pleats by placing pins 130 mm, 50 mm, 70 mm, 50 mm and repeat these measurements for the length of the material (Fig. 59d), arrange the pleats as in Fig. 59e. Baste the pleats into position and press.

6   Place the right side of the frill to the right side of the side band, arrange the pleats at the corners as C in Fig. 59a. Machine, using a piping foot.

7   Remove the tackings from the pleats; turn up 50 mm hem on to the wrong side and hem. Neaten all the raw edges, press.

STYLE NO. 2 (Fig. 60a)

For a tailored effect Style No. 2 is best made in a firm plain fabric. Allow 300 mm for a pleat in each corner of the divan. Instead of piping use a rough textured braid. Make pillow covers to match.

STYLE NO. 3

If frills are to be preferred then use them to the best advantage. Have frills on the divan, cushions and curtains. Allow 1½ times the total measurement round the divan for the frill. Do not mix up styles such as pleats, frills and pelmets in the same room.

Trunk covers

A travelling trunk can be converted into a bedroom seat by using a foam pad for the seat. The foam pad should be the size of the trunk and be covered in a cheap fabric such as calico. The loose cover is made as for a divan.

Valances

Valances are used between the mattress and the base of the bed and can be highly attractive. They can be used with a duvet or with a top cover. The colour of the valance must link with the colour of the duvet or top cover. When making a valance for a bed with posts then the valance is made in three sections; a foot and two sides. The split is not noticeable as the fullness hides the post.

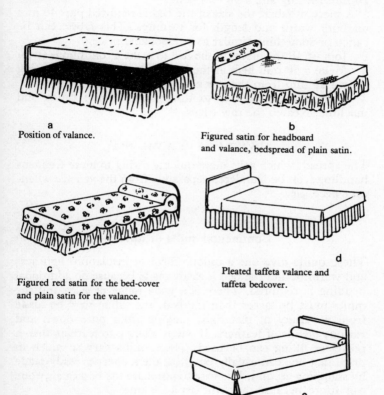

a
Position of valance.

b
Figured satin for headboard and valance, bedspread of plain satin.

c
Figured red satin for the bed-cover and plain satin for the valance.

d
Pleated taffeta valance and taffeta bedcover.

e
A very fine fabric such as linen is best for a straight valance with a pleat at the corners only. The bed-cover is of plain linen.

Figure 61

METHOD FOR FRILLED VALANCE

1   For the frill multiply the length of the bed by two, add the width and allow half as much again for the fullness. The width of fabric should be the height of the bed from the ground plus 20 mm turning and a 50 mm hem.

A piece of fabric the size of the bed is required plus 40 mm on both width and length for turnings. This fabric can be calico or something similar at a reasonable price.

2   Join up all the pieces of the frill to make a continuous strip.

3   Make a 50 mm hem at the bottom and put in a gathering thread 20 mm from the raw edge at the top.

4   Place the flounce on to three sides of the calico and machine. Neaten the raw edges.

ADVANTAGES OF A VALANCE

The spread, which soils more quickly owing to more frequent handling, can be laundered separately from the valance whenever necessary.

Continental quilts or duvets

These quilts give one a unique form of insulation, lightness and warmth, and the bed is easily made because no additional bedding is required. There is a wide range of sizes and the quilts must be larger than the bed; the filling may be made from a variety of materials, ranging from pure down and various blends of feathers. If one is allergic to feathers then a polyester filling can be used. These quilts vary so much in price that one can usually purchase them cheaper ready-made by shopping around. It is wise to purchase the best quality one can afford because they will last a lifetime.

The covers are really like making a large cushion cover with a zip part-way along one side, and the materials used should be easily washed and not crease. A polyester and cotton mixture is generally used.

110

Eiderdowns

There is very little demand for these, but one may require to repair a worn cover. The patch is best cut to form a decorative shape. Two patches could be used, one for the repair and the other for decoration. Place the patch on to the right side of the cover and hem on two sides, then attach the piping cord (this may also need recovering). Repair the back of the eiderdown in the same way.

CHAPTER 6
Carpets

Carpets give an air of luxury and comfort in a home, and also deaden sounds. They are one of the most expensive items in a home and in consequence great care should be taken in choosing them. Good quality carpets last a lifetime, with very little need of repair.

Carpets range from the highly expensive Persian and Chinese carpets, which have a sheen and softness like silk, through medium-priced wool and nylon to inexpensive rough sisal. But generally one sees fitted carpets (wall to wall) and these may vary in quality according to the purpose of the room as well as the money available. For example, a bedroom will not receive the same amount of heavy wear as a living room.

The carpet may have a rubber backing (no underlay is required in this case) or jute, and have a pile of man-made fibre, pure wool, or a mixture of the two. It is best to ask advice in the large stores about qualities because of the constant changes in the development of floor coverings. It is also important to give thought to the actual design of the carpet. A pattern does not show marks of wear or stains as easily as a plain carpet, but a plain carpet makes a room look larger.

Underfelts

When purchasing a carpet it is wise to get a good underfelt or underlay at the same time. The heavier this underlay is, the longer the life of the carpet; it gives a luxurious tread and helps to keep the carpet clean. The best underlay is one of foam rubber backed with hessian. Do not choose one which is too spongy; there are several different kinds, but some are firmer than others. Place the rubber side next to the floor with the hessian side uppermost, then lay the carpet on top.

Prepare the floor before laying the carpet; see that it is free from nails or sprigs, and clean. Wide cracks in the floor-boards should be filled in and it is worth while to make it as level as possible.

Stair carpet

The stairs should be prepared in the same way. One point worth noting is that the pile of the carpet should run down the stairs. Underfelt pads should be used or, better still, foam rubber pads. When laying the carpet, work from the bottom step upwards.

Carpet tiles

There are a number of different qualities available, and research is constantly being carried out in this field. A carpet tile may have a matt or pile surface, with a rubber backing (no underlay required). The tiles have the great advantage that they can be removed from areas of the floor which receive heavy usage and exchanged with tiles from another part of the room. It is important always to check that the direction of the pile of the tile goes in the same direction as that which is being replaced. There are arrows on the back of the tile and these help when laying. Tiles may be used in any room, including the kitchen, especially for a bachelor flat. If there is spillage then the tile can be sponged clean or lifted from the floor to be more thoroughly cleaned.

There are different pile effects which can be obtained. When laying tiles as in Fig. 62 the tiles are laid in two directions, one lot of arrows pointing towards the door and the alternate tile arrow pointing towards the unit. When laying tiles try to have whole tiles by the door or a unit which may be in constant use.

113

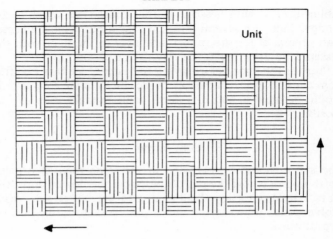

Figure 62

Carpet repairs

If rugs and carpets are badly worn, the threadbare part can be cut away and the carpet made smaller. If there is a hole, it may be patched (if there is a spare piece which matches the design) so that it is not noticeable from the right side.

PATCHING A CARPET

1   Cut away the worn area until it is either square or oblong in shape. Cut a piece of carpet to match the design (Fig. 63b) so that it will fit into the hole.

2   Using carpet tape which already has adhesive on one side, cut strips of the tape to extend beyond the hole (Fig. 63a). Pull off the protective covering from the tape and lay it half way over the carpet (Fig. 63a), working on the underside. Turn the carpet over and fit the patch into the space.

114

BINDING A CARPET

If the carpet is jute backed, then it is liable to fray unless the raw edge is treated. Use carpet tape which has adhesive on one side. Pull off the protective covering of the tape and place on to the raw edge of the carpet. If, in the course of time, the tape is found to peel away in places, a few stitches can be used to make it secure.

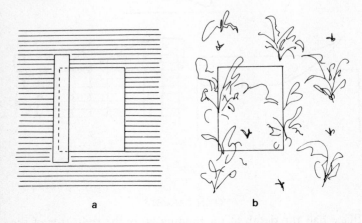

a   b

Figure 63

APPLYING BINDING WITH SOLUTION

The binding may be attached with a specially prepared solution. It is not necessary to fray the edge of the carpet before applying the binding. Spread a layer of the solution on to the back of the carpet, also on to the binding. Leave until the surfaces become tacky, then stick both edges together and leave for 24 hours. Work one row of carpet stitch (Fig. 64a) along the outer edge of the binding and the carpet; this row of stitching is necessary to prevent the edge of the pile of the carpet being sucked up by a vacuum cleaner.

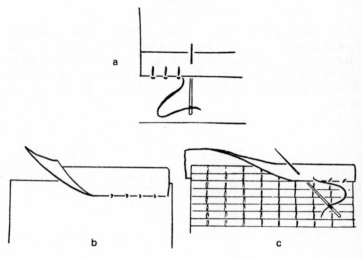

Figure 64

THIN CARPETS

Place half the depth of the binding on to the right side of the carpet and stab stitch it as in Fig. 64b. Turn over the remaining portion of webbing or binding on to the wrong side and hem (Fig. 64c).

Cutting down of carpets with borders

Very good quality carpets can be purchased in the auction rooms. They may not be the size required, but can be cut down. The border may be woven separately or woven as part of the whole carpet.

1   If the border is stitched on then unpick the border as in Fig. 65a.

2   Make the carpet the length required by cutting along the dotted line as in Fig. 65a, A-B being equal to the surplus.

116

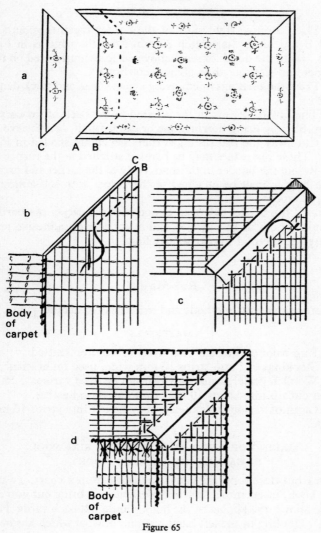

Figure 65

117

TO MAKE MITRE

1　Place the two right sides of the border together, points C and B touching. Stab stitch 20 mm from the edge as in Fig. 65b. (Note the depth of seam allowance previously used on the carpet and if larger then allow accordingly).

2　Press the turnings open, using a heavy iron and thick damp cloth.

3　The raw edges should be secured to the back of the carpet (Fig. 65c) by using herringbone or catch stitch, or adhesive.

4　Cut away the protruding corners which are shaded in Fig. 65c. These raw edges may be blanket stitched to the carpet.

5　Rejoin the border to the main body of the carpet and press. The border may be attached to the carpet with self-adhesive carpet tape.

Note: If the border is woven in one with the carpet the border should be cut as in Fig. 65a and attached with adhesive tape using the method for carpet patching.

Rug-Making

There are various methods and materials for making rugs.

MATERIALS

1　Rug wool on hessian or canvas, crochet or knitted.

2　Stockings cut into strips 10 mm wide, used on hessian.

3　Woollen undergarments which can be dyed various colours then cut up into strips 10 mm wide, used on hessian.

4　Cloth of various thicknesses may be cut into strips 10 mm wide.

MAKING OF A PILE RUG USING CUT RUG WOOL, CANVAS AND CROCHET HOOK

Mark out design on the canvas or work from a chart. To use the hook, insert into a hole in the canvas and bring out into the hole above; the latchet of the hook should fall backwards (Fig. 66a). Holding in the left hand a strand of wool which has been

doubled to make a loop, slip this over the hook (Fig. 66b). Pull
the hook towards you and the latchet will fall over the hook.
Push the hook forward through the loop (Fig. 66c), catch the
hook round the two ends held in the left hand and draw the
tool through the loop. Pull the ends of the wool tight (Fig.
66d). Continue working in this way.

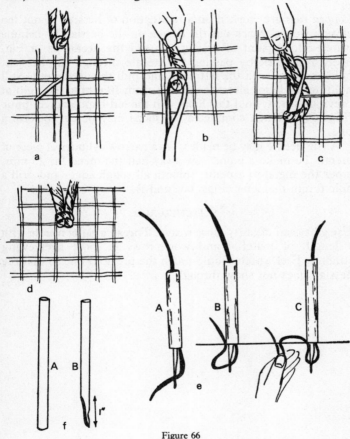

Figure 66

119

STOCKINGS

These should be sorted into groups of different colours. The design of the rug may consist of units of beige edged with a deeper colour. Commence by cutting round and round the stocking to form long continuous strips, which may be worked to form loops or stitched.

Looped rugs are worked on a foundation of hessian of not too close a weave. Mark out the design on the hessian by using a water colour paint or crayon. Thread the needle as in Fig. 66eA and work by passing the needle through the hessian; hold the loop with the left hand and pull the needle out. Still holding the loop, insert the needle again 10 mm to the right of previous stitch; hold this loop with the left hand and continue (Fig. 66e). When completed the loops may be cut to form a pile.

A rug needle may be made from a narrow cylindrical piece of metal. To make a point, saw away half the metal for 25 mm, taper the metal to a point, smooth all rough edges and drill a hole 6 mm diameter (Figs. 66e and f).

STITCHED RUG

Use a hessian of fairly loose weave. Thread a raffia needle with a length of material and work rows of loose oversewing stitches. Each stitch should touch the previous one so that the hessian does not show through.

CHAPTER 7
Lampshades

No scheme of soft furnishing is complete without a lampshade or shades to harmonise with the type of decoration chosen. Lampshades can be inexpensively made. Odd scraps of furnishing fabric can be used in conjunction with either new or old frames. In this chapter only a few methods of making are given, but many original ideas can be carried out with the aid of the information given. Table lamps may be made from empty bottles, jars, vases, candlesticks, etc.

A lampshade must bear some relation to the base (e.g. a dainty lace lampshade for a cut-glass vase base). If using a wine bottle for the base, try to collect a variety of labels from other bottles and stick on to a paper or vellum lampshade. The size and shape must be correct for the base; it is often advisable to take the base with you when purchasing the lampshade frame. This gives you a better opportunity to see the correct relationship between the base and the shade. Time can be well spent on a visit to the lighting department of an exclusive store, where one can easily see how the size of lampshade varies with the size of the base.

Materials

Crinothene is a washable plastic obtainable in a variety of colours and 86 cm wide. Suitable for most styles of lampshades.
Types of decoration: A special type of transfer can be used. Oil paints, fancy plastic, thonging, braids and fringe.
Vellum White or Natural, sold by the sheet.

Types of decoration: It can be decorated in the same way as crinothene, and painted with clear varnish which gives a rich finish. Floral designs or cuttings from nursery books can be cut out and stuck on to the vellum.

Buckram is a stiff fabric obtainable mostly in white; it is 60 cm wide and is sold by the metre.

Types of decoration: Fancy stitching, braids, thonging, ribbons; it can be painted or varnished.

Fabrics Light weights only, such as printed cotton, artificial silks, shantung, glazed chintz, furnishing satin, moiré. Before attempting to make a lampshade in material, place it close to an electric light bulb to see what reaction the light has on the colour and pattern of the fabric.

Transparent fabrics Organdie, nylon, voile, and many other kinds of transparent material can be used, but the style of the lampshade should be simple. These shades will have to be lined to be of any use other than decoration. The material used for lining should be thicker than the top cover – buckram is very suitable. If the lamp is to be used for reading or sewing, the colour of the lining should be white so that the light is clear. To obtain a warm effect use colours such as pink, beige, peach, etc. Strong blues and greens should be avoided, as they make anyone sitting near the light look ill.

String or yarn Coloured string or thick knitting yarns may be used to cover a lampshade frame. The style of the frame must be angular (i.e. without curves). Commence at the top of the frame and wind the string or yarn round the frame and secure the end of the string at the lower edge.

An adjustable six-hole leather punch is required for the making of a large number of shades.

'Empire' lampshade

The frame for this can be a one-piece frame with rigid struts (Fig. 67a); a two-piece pendant type (Fig. 67b); a two-piece reversible, gimbal type (Fig. 67c). The height of the two-piece lampshade can be varied to any size.

PATTERN FOR 'EMPIRE' SHADE (Fig. 67d)

A to B is a vertical line, length about 460 cm. C can be any
distance from A, because A is not permanently fixed.

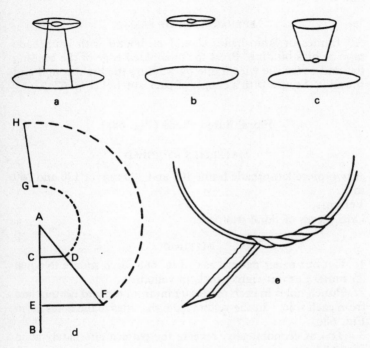

Figure 67

C to D is the radius of the top ring, measured at right angles to
A to B line (for a 100 mm diameter ring, measure 50 mm). E to
C is the height of shade. E to F is the radius of the bottom
ring, measured at right angles to A to B line (for 200 mm
diameter ring, measure 100 mm). Rule line from F through D
until it touches the line A to B. When the two lines meet put a
dot and use this for the compass point.

Describe an arc from D to G which is equal to the circumference of the top ring. Describe an arc from F to H which is equal to the circumference of the bottom ring. Rule line G to H.

PREPARATION OF FRAME

All frames of lampshades should be bound with lampshade tape or bias binding. Press the one folded edge of the binding flat and cover the wire frame by winding the braid round and round it. Secure with a couple of back stitches (Fig. 67e).

Floral fluted shade (Fig. 68a)

MATERIALS REQUIRED

A two-piece lampshade frame 100 and 200 mm or 130 and 260 mm.
Vellum.
Odd pieces of floral wallpaper.

METHOD

1 Cut out paper pattern as in Fig. 68b (each square to equal 25 mm). Cut out eight panels in vellum.
2 Punch holes in each panel 20 mm from top and bottom and from each side. Cut the vellum from the sides to the holes, as in Fig. 68c.
3 To cut economically, reverse the pattern alternately as in Fig. 68d.
4 Cut out floral motifs from wallpaper and stick to vellum.
5 Varnish all the panels with clear varnish and leave to dry for 24 hours.
6 Join all the flutes together with the narrow parts uppermost, either by (a) machining on an ordinary sewing machine, or (b) stapling with an office stapling machine, or (c) using paper fasteners (the pronged type), which are pushed through the paper and opened out.

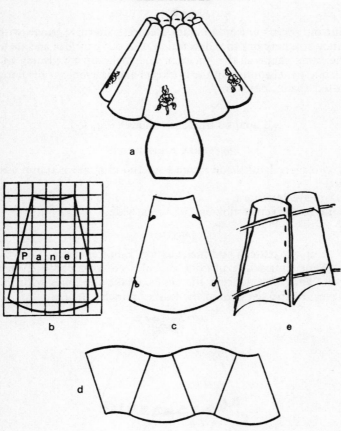

Figure 68

7   Fit the shade on to the frame by slipping the wire through the slits into the holes in vellum (Fig. 68e).
Note: Nursery motifs could be used in the place of floral ones.
   This style is suitable for a standard lamp.

125

ALTERNATIVE STYLES

Cut the panels out of buckram, decorate alternate panels with fancy stitchery or other decoration. Cut out panels of acetate to the same shape as the buckram and make up by placing the acetate panels on top of the buckram and assemble as for floral fluted shade, nos 6 to 7.

Thonged buckram shade (Fig. 69)

MATERIALS REQUIRED

A two-piece lampshade frame with 100 mm and 200 mm size rings.
0.5 metre buckram.
3 metres of velvet ribbon 15-20 mm wide.

METHOD

1 Cut out pattern and make as for 'Empire' shade.
2 Pencil mark the position of holes on wrong side 20 mm apart and 20 mm from the edges. Make the holes with the largest of the six sizes in the leather punch.

Figure 69

3 Cut one length of ribbon 43 cm long for the bow, and a length of 90 cm for the top edge; the remainder is used for the lower edge.

4 Twist one end of ribbon to give it a point and thong round the edge of the lamp shade, securing the metal ring to the buckram in the same operation. (Thonging is only over-sewing.)

5 Finish thonging on the wrong side by stitching the two ends of the velvet together.

6 Make 43 cm piece of ribbon into a bow and stitch to top edge.

Note: A fancy cord (or rug wool) may be used for thonging but do not use anything thinner than velvet ribbon because buckram cuts into it.

Fancy thonged lampshade (Fig. 70a)

MATERIALS REQUIRED

Two-piece wire frame. 100 and 200 mm size.

0.5 metre buckram or crinothene.

1 skein each of three different colours of candlewick cotton.

METHOD

1 Cut out and make up as for 'Empire' shade.

2 Mark position of punch-holes with pencil on wrong side on lower edge only. The first row is 30 mm from edge and 25 mm apart. Second row 25 mm from edge and 15 mm apart (Fig. 70b).

3 Thong with one coloured cotton through every other hole, on the bottom row (Fig. 70b).

4 Thong the second colour through the remaining holes in the bottom row (Fig. 70c).

5 Thong with third colour through top row of holes, thonging in the opposite direction (Fig. 70d).

6 Twist two of the colours together to form a cord and stitch to top edge.

LAMPSHADES

ALTERNATIVE STYLE 1

Make up an 'Empire' style lampshade with buckram, cut out leaf or flower motifs of furnishing fabric, arrange on the buckram and stick with paste. Cut out a piece of acetate the same shape as the shade. Cover the shade with it and stitch to the lower edge by oversewing. Bind the outer edge with plain material used in the furnishing scheme.

Note: Autumn leaves, seaweed and sprays of fern may be used in place of material motifs.

ALTERNATIVE STYLE 2

Make up as for 'Empire' style in buckram, then cover with furnishing fabric by rolling and stretching a piece of fabric round the shade. Pin the material to the top and bottom rings of the shade frame. Cut off material 15 mm beyond the pins. Turn under the raw edge down the side and join together by hemming. Turn in the raw edge at the top and bottom of material and hem, finishing with a braid.

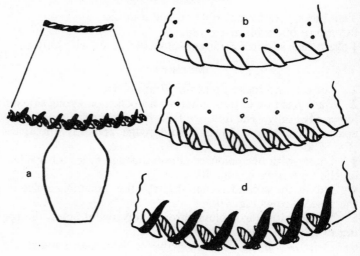

Figure 70

Straight fluted shade (Fig. 71a)

MATERIALS REQUIRED

A two-piece lampshade frame 150 and 250 mm.
0.6 metre buckram.
8 metres of narrow ribbon.

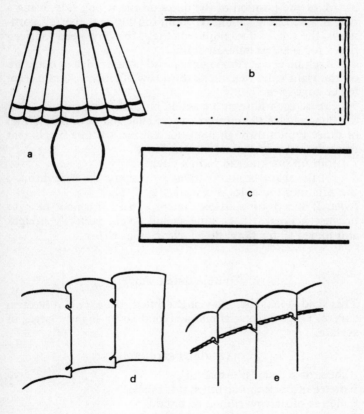

Figure 71

129

LAMPSHADES

METHOD

1   Cut two strips of buckram 240 mm deep of the same width as the sheet (if other material is used the length should be 1½ times the circumference of the lower ring, or twice the circumference if deeper flutes are required).

2   Join the two right sides of buckram together by machining 10 mm from the edge (Fig. 71b).

3   Mark the position of the flutes on the wrong side, using a pencil. Each flute should be 90 mm to 110 mm apart, according to the size of flute required (Fig. 71b). You need fourteen flutes for the 250 mm size frame.

4   Machine velvet ribbon on top and bottom edge of buckram on the right side. Machine a third row of ribbon 30 mm from lower edge (Fig. 71c).

5   Crease each flute into position on the wrong side.

6   Punch holes 30 mm from the top edge and 10 mm from fold of flute. Punch through both thicknesses. Cut the parchment from the sides to the holes (Fig. 71d).

7   Join up buckram to form a circle.

8   Fit the shade on to the frame by slipping the wire through the slits into the holes provided (Fig. 71e).

Note: If sheepskin split parchment is used it cannot be bent because it breaks. Each flute should be cut perfectly straight and joined as for floral fluted shade (Fig. 68).

Double fluted shade

This shade looks like the straight fluted shade, only it has two covers. One of material and a second cover slightly larger of acetate.

MATERIALS REQUIRED

1 sheet of acetate (transparent).
1 metre of buckram or other stiff fabric.
8 metres of narrow ribbon or braid.
A two-piece lampshade frame 150 and 250 mm.

130

METHOD

Work from 1 to 8 of the method for straight fluted shade, omitting No. 4.

9   Cut out the acetate the depth of the buckram and the length of the buckram strip plus 25 mm extra for every flute.

10   Make up as for straight fluted shade from Nos 2 to 7, but when measuring the position of the flutes add 25 mm on to every flute (e.g. if the flutes of the buckram are 90 mm then the flutes of the outer cover should be at least 110 mm).

11   Fit the shade on to the frame by slipping the wire through the slits into the holes provided.

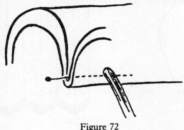

Figure 72

12   Place a plain pin down the fold and through the binding on the wire frame. Do this to each flute. The pins remain in position (Fig. 72).

Note: This style of lampshade is suitable for standard lamps, but the depths of the flutes and height of shade would be greater.

The buckram or acetate may be painted to give a pretty effect.

Pleated shade (Fig. 73a)

MATERIALS REQUIRED

A lampshade frame with 100 mm and 200 mm, or 120 mm and 250 mm rings.
0.5 metre of glazed chintz 76 cm wide.

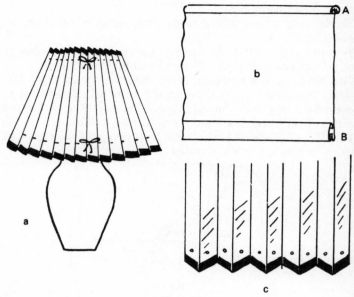

Figure 73

3 metres of cotton bias binding matching the deepest shade in chintz.
1 skein of thick embroidery cotton or Star Sylko no. 3.
4 large beads.

Note: If a large lampshade is made, the material should be 40 mm deeper than the depth of the frame. The length of material should be at least twice the circumference of lower edge of frame.

METHOD

1   Cut out and join up glazed chintz by overlapping one selvedge over the other, and machine down both edges. If there is a raw edge turn it in and press before lapping it over. Always join by a straight thread.

132

2   Attach bias binding. At top edge, the binding should be folded lengthwise with the raw edge of chintz inside the fold (Fig. 73b). Tack firmly and then machine through all thicknesses.

3   Place right sides of binding to wrong side of chintz on the lower edge. Machine and press the seam open. Turn the binding completely over on to the right side as for a facing and machine the top edge (Fig. 73b).

4   Lay the strip out flat, wrong side uppermost. Mark the position of pleats 10 mm apart for shades 200 mm in diameter and 15 mm for larger shades.

5   Fold sharply from each mark on the left hand side to the corresponding mark on the right. Fold inwards and outwards, concertina fashion. Crease each fold well and make sure it is on a straight thread (Fig. 73c).

6   Punch holes through the pleats on wrong side 15 mm from the top edge and 25 mm from the lower edge. Two or three pleats may be punched at a time. To keep them all level mark the position of holes with a pencil dot or make a template.

7   Join up the pleated strip to form a circle.

8   Thread the cord through the holes on the right side. Place a bead on either end of thread and secure with a knot to prevent it falling off.

9   Place shade on wire frame. Draw up the cords to fit and tie in a bow.

10   The shade may be stitched to the frame at each pleat or left loose, and it will not fall off.

Spotted muslin fluted shade (Fig. 74a)

MATERIALS REQUIRED

0.5 metre buckram.
0.5 metre spotted muslin or silk.
7 metres ribbon 25 mm wide.
A metal ring 150 mm diameter and another 100 mm with gimbal attached.

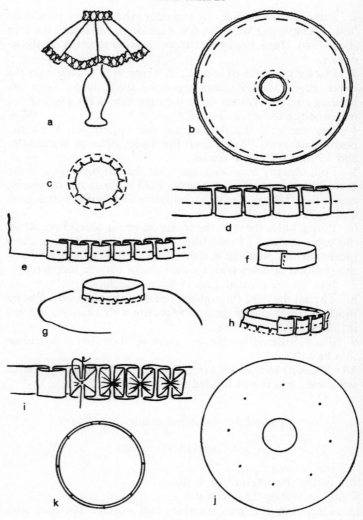

Figure 74

METHOD

1   Cut a circle of buckram 460 mm in diameter.

2   Cover with muslin and tack the two together 10 mm from the edge of buckram. Cut away the surplus muslin level with the buckram.

3   Find the centre of the circle. Draw a circle 55 mm in radius from this point. Tack the muslin and buckram together 10 mm from this line and machine. Cut out the 55 mm radius circle as in Fig. 74b.

4   Snip the raw edge of muslin and buckram down to the machine stitching (Fig. 74c) and bend the edges upwards.

5   Pleat the ribbon as in Fig. 74d. Make 25 mm wide pleats and tack down the centre of the ribbon. Tack the pleated ribbon, extending it 10 mm beyond the edge of buckram on the outer edge of circle and machine (Fig. 74e).

6   Cut a piece of buckram 20 mm deep and the circumference of the 100 mm ring (330 mm) and 10 mm, overlap the raw edges of the buckram 10 mm and stitch by hand (Fig. 74f).

7   Slip the small ring of buckram into the centre of the large circle of buckram; the snipped edges should be on the outside of the buckram. Stitch the buckram to the snipped edge by hand (Fig. 74g).

8   Stitch a length of pleated ribbon to the centre of the buckram as in Fig. 74h.

9   The centre pleats of the ribbon may be stitched to form a rosette as in Fig. 74i.

10   The metal ring (100 mm in diameter) should be stitched to the top edge of buckram (Fig. 74h).

11   Turn the large circle of muslin-covered buckram on to the wrong side. Divide the circle into eight and mark with a pencil dot 75 mm from the edge (Fig. 74j).

12   Mark the 150 mm metal ring into 8 by first marking the halves, quarters and eighths as in Fig. 74k.

13   Stitch the dot marks on the buckram to the dot marks on the metal ring. The space between the dots on the buckram is greater than the space on the metal ring and it is this difference that causes the flutes.

Curtain material lampshades (Fig. 75a)

MATERIALS REQUIRED

A lampshade frame.
An odd scrap of material to match the curtains.
Odd pieces of cream material for lining.

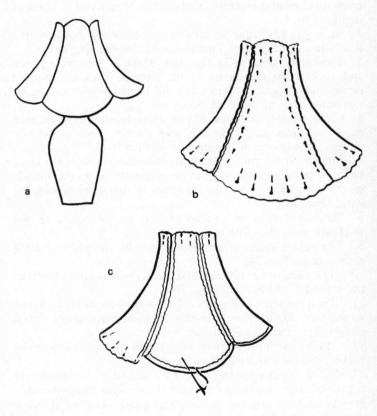

Figure 75

METHOD

1 Cut out a paper pattern of one panel of the lampshade. The pattern can be made by pinning the paper on to the frame and pencil marking the exact shape on paper.

2 Cut out the necessary number of panels for the shade, keeping the centre of each panel on a straight thread. Leave 10 mm turnings.

3 Pin each section separately on to the frame, at both top and bottom edges. The point of the pins should always point at the centre of the panel. Pin seams carefully as in Fig. 75b.

4 Mark one of the panels of the lampshade frame with a tacking cotton and mark the same panel on the cover so that they can be matched again.

5 Remove the cover from the frame, but do not remove the pins from the seams. Tack the panels together and try on the frame again to make sure it fits. Machine the seams and press the turnings open.

6 Place the shade on to the frame and pin carefully top and bottom. Turn up the raw edge and hem to the frame (Fig. 75c).

7 Make the top cover in the same way, only turn the top cover right side out so that all the raw edges are inside.

8 Fit on to the lampshade frame; pin carefully, turn in the raw edges at top and bottom and hem to the frame.

Note: This method can only be used if the frame is not shaped very much.

ALTERNATIVE STYLE (LACE)

This must have a material foundation. Make up as for 1 to 6. Pin on the lace and stretch to the seams of the under cover, stitch to the under cover and trim away any surplus lace. Use braid to hide the joins.

ALTERNATIVE METHOD (UNLINED)

Pin the material on to a panel of the lampshade, keeping the straight thread down the centre of the panel, and cut out to the shape required allowing 10 mm turnings. Turn under the raw edge and pin to the frame and secure to the latter by small stitches. Cover each panel in the same way. For some shapes of shades it might be better to cut on the cross; pin one panel with the material on the straight and one panel on the cross, then decide which is the better fit.

Empire shade with balloon lining

Shades are often made of a soft fabric and look much nicer when lined. A crepe-backed satin may be used for the lining.

METHOD

Prepare an Empire style frame as on page 122.

1 Fold the fabric in half by placing the selvedges together and right side inside (Fig. 76a). Fold again (Fig. 76b). Place this fold to one strut of the frame and pin at top and bottom (Fig. 76c).

2 Open back half of the fabric (Fig. 76d). Pin through the two layers and the binding on the frame, pins pointing inwards. Continue pinning the fabric to the frame every 10 mm. Pull firmly to make it smooth. When the next strut is reached pin the fabric to it until half of the frame is covered. This takes quite a time because it will be necessary to keep adjusting the pins to obtain a tight, smooth effect, and keeping the grain straight.

3 Mark the top and bottom of the frame with pencil dots before removing the pins. Tack the two pieces of fabric together (using small stitches) down the side of the struts. Continue the stitching a little above and below the rings of the frame (Fig. 76e). Machine the seams and cut turnings to 5 mm, but allow 30 mm at top and bottom of shade. Press turnings open.

4 Slip the cover on to the frame with right side of fabric uppermost. The seams should be directly over the struts. Pin

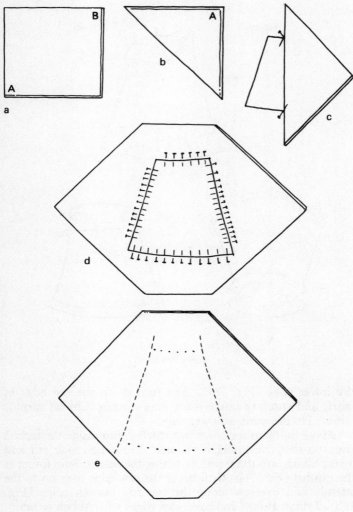

Figure 76 (a-e)

139

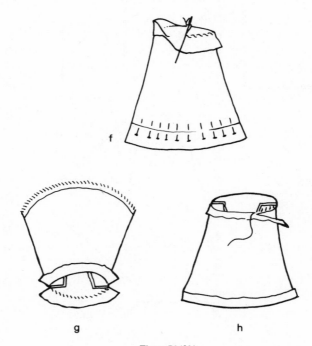

Figure 76 (f-h)

the lower edge (Fig. 76f), then turn down the top edge of fabric and stitch to frame using long stitches. Cut off surplus fabric. Do the same at lower edge.

5   Make lining as for cover but stitch 2 mm inside the tacked seam so that the lining is smaller. Turn right side out and insert lining into the frame matching the seams. Snip lining at the gimbal (Fig. 76g) then bring the raw edge over on to the outside and oversew along the top and bottom edges (Fig. 76h). Trim turnings and cover raw edges with ribbon or braid, etc.

140

Finishing of lampshades

The type of edging chosen for finishing or trimming a lamp-shade depends upon the type of shade and furnishings in the room.

1 A rich effect can be obtained by using expensive braids, tasselled and ordinary fringes, on shades made of rich furnishing fabrics such as satin, moiré silk, etc.

2 A dainty finish is obtained by pleating ribbon in different ways for shades made of organdie, ninon, nylon, etc.

3 It is often difficult to link up the colours of a room with the lamp, or the base of the lampstand with the shade. This can be largely overcome by one of the following methods:

(a) Bind the edge of the shade with some of the material used for making the furnishings. Details of binding in Fig. 73b.

(b) A plait can be made from a skein of cheap cotton yarn of the required colour.

(c) A twisted cord can be made of embroidery wool. To obtain a perfect match take a strand out of the pile of the carpet, or a scrap of furnishing fabric, or take the lampstand, or whatever is required to be matched, to an embroidery shop and match with tapestry wools.

TO MAKE A PLAIT FROM A SKEIN OF YARN

1 Cut the yarn into lengths sufficient to go round the circumference 1½ times.

2 Tie the ends together at one end, then divide into three equal parts as in Fig. 77.

3 Bring A over to B (Fig. 77b) then C over A (Fig. 77c); continue bringing the outer group of threads first from the right and then from the left towards the centre (Fig. 77d).

4 Attach to lampshade, using small stitches on the right side and long stitches on the wrong side.

CORDS

To make a three-core cord (Fig. 78) three different colours of wool are required (Fig. 78b). Nine strands of each colour are

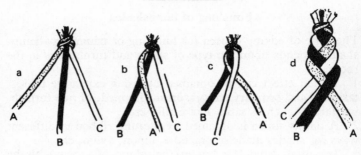

Figure 77

required for each core. They must be of equal length and
measure 1½ times the circumference of the lampshade. The
nine strands are twisted together and to do this, two people are

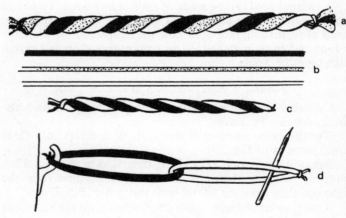

Figure 78

required (we will name them A and B), who hold the respective
ends of the cord. A twists in a clockwise direction and B in an
anti-clockwise direction. When the first core is tightened, the

142

ends are placed under their respective feet, keeping the core taut. The second and third core are twisted in a like manner. When the second core is completed this can also be placed under the feet. On completion of the third one, the other two are picked up. A ties the three ends together and B does likewise and releases her end as she does so. A gives the whole three cores a quick shake, and they will twist on their own and so form a cord. It is then ready to stitch on a lampshade as for a cord on a cushion (Fig. 11).

Note: If the three cores of the cord appear loosely twisted together this is due to insufficient twisting of each core in the first place and cord can be undone and re-twisted.

TWO-CORE CORD (Fig. 78c)

Take four lengths of tapestry wool, sufficient to go round the circumference of the lampshade 2½ times. Fold in two and put a knot in the end. Take another four lengths of a different colour. Thread this through the loop formed by the previous wool and tie a knot in the end. Place a drawing pin through one knot and firmly secure to a piece of wood or place the knot over a hook. Pass a pencil partly through the other end (Fig. 78d), rotate the pencil, at the same time keeping the wool taut; continue until it is tight. With the left hand take hold of the centre where the two colours meet, with the right hand grasp hold of the two knots; let go of the middle and shake the cord and it will twist itself. Secure by knotting the two ends together.

Note: The number of strands required and the length depends upon the thickness of the strands and twisting. The greater the number of strands the greater the length required.

CHAPTER 8
Upholstery

The earliest form of upholstery consisted of a piece of leather stretched across two pieces of wood. This has gradually been developed through the ages so that now we have a variety of upholstery methods including latex foam seats and cushions moulded from rubber.

Upholstery is really the improvement of furniture intended for relaxation, such as chairs, stools, settees and beds. Basically, they all have to have a firm foundation of webbing (or wood for ottomans and slipper boxes) covered with a springy padding of hair, springs or latex foam. Even a divan bed is really an elongated sprung stool, with a mattress of rubber or a spring mattress similar to a spring interior cushion.

Upholstery is concerned not only with the making of new items of furniture, but with the repairing of existing pieces. In this chapter the basic forms of all types of seats have been dealt with, from the more traditional type of seat comprising webbing, springs and stuffing to the modern tension spring with latex foam cushion.

No section on upholstery would be complete without some mention of the treatment of wood. This has been lightly dealt with.

Upholstery materials

Webbing is placed across the open framework of seats, and there are two different kinds; one is made of jute and is either black and white (old-English) or jute colour. It is 50 mm wide, providing a firm base to upholster upon. The other is rubberised webbing called Pirelli, and this can be obtained in various widths, 35 mm and 55 mm are the most common. It is extremely strong and is used stretched or tensioned to give a firm but elastic seat and is often used to replace springs when re-upholstering old furniture. The main padding of the seat would be made of deep latex foam.

Springs may be used in the seats, backs and arms of chairs, and are made in a number of sizes to meet various requirements. The springs have a coating of copper to prevent rusting and rotting of webbing and canvas.

Hessian is a product from jute, the better qualities being light in colour and fine in texture. It is 183 cm wide and is used to cover the springs.

Scrim is a very fine canvas or form of hessian, used to cover the first stuffing.

Calico is used as a final covering before the outer cover is put on. It can be purchased in various widths, 102-27 cm and 183 cm.

Wadding (thick upholstery) is very thick and can be used to replace one layer of stuffing. It is sold by the metre.

Horse-hair is used for first stuffings. A high grade of hair is white, and the actual hairs are very long. Other grades of hair usually contain a percentage of hog-hair which is very short and difficult to handle. The natural springiness of hair makes it a better stuffing than fibre.

Coir is a trade name for coconut fibre. It should be free of dust. The longer the strands of fibre the better the quality.

Rubberised hair is sold by the sheet 910 × 1820 mm, and 25 or 50 mm thick.

Laid cord is similar to very thick string and is sold in 500 gm balls.

Twine is sold in 25 gm balls and is made in a variety of thicknesses. It is used for the stitching of edges.

Tacks are sold in 250 and 500 gm packs. Size 16 mm 'improved' is the size used for attaching webbing and canvas to chairs; 12 mm size for stools; 12-15 mm 'fine' are used for attaching hessian, etc.

Latex foam comes in many sizes and thicknesses (see p. 165).

COVERINGS FOR UPHOLSTERED CHAIRS AND STOOLS

Covering for upholstered furniture should be of a fairly hard-wearing fabric such as tapestry, moquette, bedford cord, tweed, heavy quality damasks, etc. Subdued colours are most suitable as they do not show marks of dirt so easily. Avoid all thin fabrics, which soon become soiled and shabby.

Tools and how to use them

A few tools only are required for upholstery; nevertheless it is very important that the correct tool for the job is known and used. The incorrect use of tools often damages them and makes the job in hand appear much more difficult. In purchasing tools, it is a penny-wise and pound-foolish policy to purchase them cheaply; it pays in the long run to get good-quality tools as they last a lifetime.

UPHOLSTERER'S HAMMER

This has a slender shaft and slender shaped head, one side of which is pronged for use in the extraction of tacks (Fig. 79a).

Grasp the hammer firmly in the right hand near the end of the shaft. All movement for driving comes from the wrist only. To drive in a tack or nail, hold the tack firmly between the thumb and first finger of the left hand, hit the tack lightly to centre it in the wood, remove the left hand and with one or two good hits, the tack can be driven home (Fig. 79b).

Note: When the left hand is otherwise engaged press the tack in with the right thumb, then use the hammer.

TACK REMOVER OR RIPPING CHISEL

This has a pronged piece of steel, the tip of which is curved, and a wooden handle attached. This tool is used to remove old covers and tacks. Usually a mallet is used to give more force to the chisel (Fig. 80a).

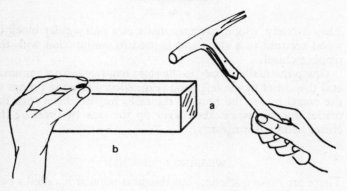

Figure 79

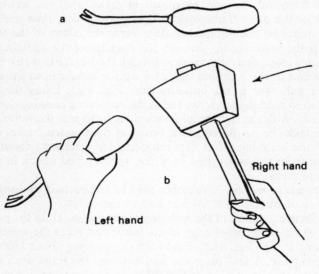

Right hand

Left hand

Figure 80

MALLET

This is really a light hammer made of a rectangular block of wood secured to a shaft and is used in conjunction with the ripping chisel.

Grasp the mallet firmly in the right hand, as with a hammer, and the chisel in the left hand (Fig. 80b). Place the prongs of the chisel under the head of the tack, hit the chisel with the mallet once or twice, then lever up the tack by pressing the chisel handle downwards.

WEBBING STRETCHER

There are many varieties, but the most popular is called a bat. It is made of wood and has a short peg attached by a chain or twine (Fig. 81a).

The stretcher, as its name implies, is used to stretch the webbing to make it taut. First secure one end of the webbing to the frame of the seat by means of tacks. Pull the webbing across the open framework to the opposite side, then use the stretcher by placing the handle towards the centre of the seat; pull the webbing up through the opening of the stretcher to form a loop, then slip the peg through the loop (Fig. 81b). Pull the end of the webbing tight, lift up the handle from the seat and pull over to the opposite side (Fig. 81c). Using the left hand to hold the stretcher and at the same time pressing downwards, with the right hand knock three tacks into the webbing, the tacks being placed in the centre of the wooden frame. Cut off the webbing (after first removing the stretcher) about 25 mm from the tacks, fold back the webbing and knock in two more tacks.

Alternative method A stretcher may be improvised by using a piece of wood 150 × 70 mm and 15 mm thick.

Secure one end of the webbing to the frame. Hold the piece of wood at the other edge of the frame and place the webbing over the top (Fig. 81d). Fold back the webbing about 230 mm from point A and place the fold between the framework and the piece of wood (as in Fig. 81e). Hold the wood in the left

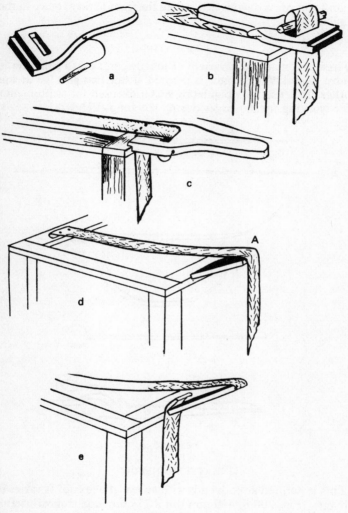

Figure 81

hand and press downwards, using the right hand to drive in the tacks.

REGULATORS

These are made in a variety of lengths, but a 255 mm one is most useful. A regulator is pointed at one end and flat at the other. It is used for regulating materials used for stuffing and for working up the edges during stitching (Fig. 82a).

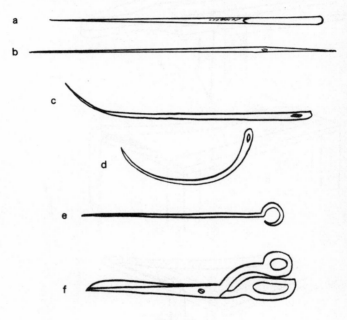

Figure 82

MATTRESS NEEDLE

This is pointed at both ends with an eye at one end. It varies in length from 200 to 460 mm but a 255 mm one is most useful. The needle is used for the stitching of edges (Fig. 82b).

SPRING NEEDLE

This is bent at one end and is also known as a sail needle. It is used for the stitching of springs (Fig. 82c).

CURVED NEEDLE OR SEMI-CIRCULAR NEEDLE

These are made in a large variety of sizes; the 60 mm and 40 mm sizes are most useful. They are used for sewing on cord and seaming on surround work (Fig. 82d).

SKEWERS

These can be obtained in 75 to 125 mm lengths. They are used instead of pins to hold covers in a temporary position (Fig. 82e).

SHEARS

Required for cutting the webbing and materials. The shears should have at least a 150 mm blade (Fig. 82f).

GIMLET

This is made of metal with a wooden handle and is somewhat like a corkscrew.

SCREWDRIVER

A screwdriver has a blunt-ended blade made of steel attached to a wooden or plastic handle.

HOW TO USE A GIMLET AND SCREWDRIVER

When you have found the desired position for the screw, you use a gimlet to make a small hole into which the screw is inserted to give it a start (Fig. 83a and b). Place the point of the gimlet at the point where a screw is to be inserted, and turn in a clockwise direction (left to right). For short screws two or three turns only of the gimlet will be necessary. Before inserting the screw rub it on ordinary washing soap or grease to enable it to go in more easily, and prevent rust. Place the screw in the hole formed, put the blade of the screwdriver into the slot on the screw and turn in a clockwise direction (Fig. 83c). *Note:* The blade of a screwdriver should not be smaller than the width of the head of the screw, otherwise the head of the screw will become chewed and will be nearly impossible to put in or remove with a screwdriver. If this happens, use a pair of pincers to remove the screw and start again with the correct size of screwdriver and a new screw.

TYPE OF SCREWS

1 Dome head: This type of screw has a slightly raised head and is used on curtain fittings (Fig. 83f and h).

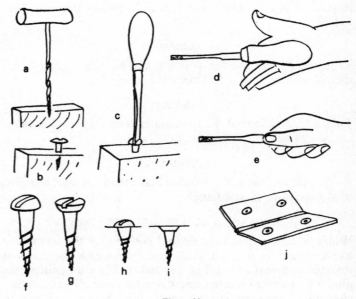

Figure 83

2 Countersunk: This type of screw has a flat head and when placed into the wood should be flush or level with it (Fig. 83g and i). After making the hole for the screw with the gimlet, you

make a wide taper for the screw head to sink into. This is usually done with a rose or countersink bit.

Hinges are attached by countersunk screws. The hinge plate is countersunk so that the head of the screw fits flush with the metal (Fig. 83j).

Sprung seat

POSITION OF WEBBING

The space between each piece of webbing should not be wider than the width of the webbing.

Measure the width of the seat and divide it by the width of the webbing and if it comes to an uneven number then there will be a space and a piece of webbing alternately (Fig. 84a). If the number is even then place a piece of webbing in the centre of the seat and place other pieces at equal distances apart (Fig. 84b).

ATTACHING OF WEBBING

1 Place the raw edge of the webbing on the inner edge of the stool and secure with three tacks (12 mm for stools, 16 mm for chairs) (Fig. 84c). Fold back the webbing and place in two more tacks (Fig. 84d).

2 Stretch the webbing across the open frame, using a webbing stretcher (Fig. 81). Place all the webbing across in one direction.

3 Place the webbing across in the other direction so that it interlaces alternately (Fig. 84e).

4 Mark out the position of the springs, which should be placed on double webbing; this is essential for extra strength (Fig. 84f). Each spring must be secured in four places to the webbing with laid cord, using a bent spring needle.

5 Make a slip-knot on the end of the cord and secure it to the webbing by taking a stitch into the webbing and slipping the needle through the loop of the knot and pull tight. Insert the needle down close to the wire of the spring (Fig. 85a). Return

again close to the wire, leaving a loop of cord (Fig. 85b). Twist the loop twice round the point of the needle (Fig. 85c). Insert the needle back into the webbing (Fig. 85d) and bring the needle up again for next stitch.

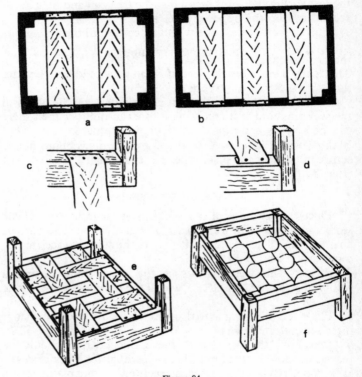

Figure 84

LASHING OF SPRINGS

1   Place a 12 mm tack (16 mm for a chair) opposite the centre of each spring. Drive it in only temporarily, that is not right the way in.

154

2   Cut a length of laid cord twice the width of the seat. When securing the laid cord to the first spring, leave sufficient cord to reach down to the frame and return to the top coil. The cord should be secured to the second coil of the first spring and then to the outer coils (Fig. 85e) of the remaining springs, except for the last spring, which is secured at the first coil and then at the second coil on the opposite side.

3   Pull down the ends of the lashing cord until the springs are upright, twist the cord round the tack, and drive down so that the head secures the cord firmly.

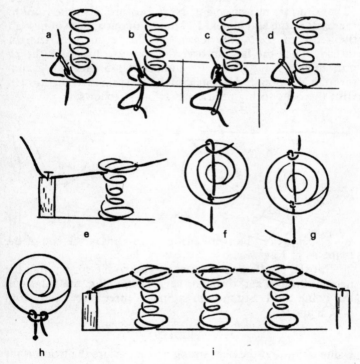

Figure 85

4   Now take the remaining ends of the laid cord and fasten them to the top coil of spring.

Fig. 85e shows the tack driven half-way into the wood. Fig. 85 f and g show the type of lashing used to prevent slipping. Figure 85h shows the knot used for fastening off. The springs must be lashed from front to back of the seat and from side to side (Fig. 85i).

HESSIAN COVER

Measure from side to side of the seat over the springs and add 50 mm to this measurement. Next measure from the front to the back of the seat and add 50 mm. Cut out a piece of hessian the required size. The hessian should be cut to a straight thread. Place the hessian over the springs, turn back the 25 mm turnings and drive 10 mm tacks (15 mm for chairs) through the double hessian. Stitch the springs to the hessian with the bent spring needle and twine as follows:

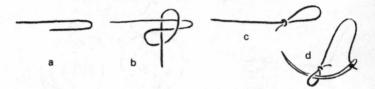

Figure 86

1   To fasten on the twine make a slip-knot in the end of the twine as in Fig. 86a, b and c.
2   Put the needle into the hessian near to the spring, pull the needle through and through the slip-knot (Fig. 86d) and pull the twine tight. Stitch each spring in three places as in Fig. 87a, b and c.

BRIDLES

Using twine and the bent spring needle, secure the twine as for previous stitching about 50 mm away from the edge of the

156

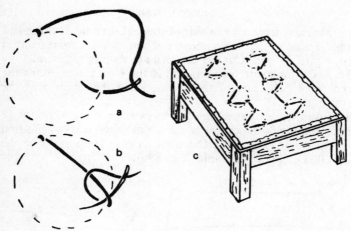

Figure 87

hessian. Take large stitches 75 to 100 mm in length, all round the seat (Fig. 88a). Another row should be made across the top or centre of the seat. Pick over the stuffing of hair or fibre carefully to remove any lumps. Place small portions part way through the bridles round the edge of the seat (Fig. 88b) and keep the stuffing evenly distributed. Repeat the process across the centre row of stitches. Fill in all spaces and cover the bridles with a thin layer of stuffing.

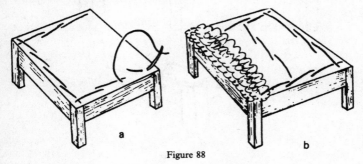

Figure 88

157

SCRIM COVER

1   Measure from side to side of the seat over the stuffing and add 25 mm to this measurement. Then measure from front to back plus 25 mm. Cut out the scrim to a straight thread.

2   Mark the centre of each side of the stool frame. Mark the centre of each side of the scrim. Place the scrim over the stuffing.

3   Commence by turning up the raw edge of the scrim for 12 mm, then tack the centre of the scrim to the marked position on the frame (Fig. 89a). Drive the tacks in temporarily on the bevelled edge of the frame (Fig. 89b).

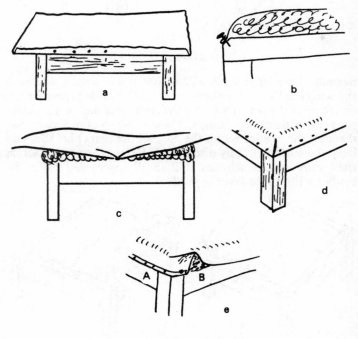

Figure 89

4 Attach the opposite side of scrim to the frame and continue by keeping the respective edges together (Fig. 89c).

5 Turn the corner by bringing the edge of the material round from side A to side B and drive in a tack (Fig. 89e), then bring the top of the corner down and drive in a tack (use 12 mm tacks on stools, 15 mm on chairs) (Fig. 89d).

6 Check over the evenness of the stuffing, then drive home all the tacks.

BLIND STITCHING (Fig. 90a, b, c, and d)

1 Using twine and a mattress needle, commence by putting a slip-knot in the end of the twine and bring the needle through the scrim about 25 mm from the left-hand corner.

2 Push the needle into the scrim at an angle of 45 degrees; the point of entry should be as near the tacks as is possible (Fig. 90a).

3 Pull the needle through until you can see the eye.

4 Push the needle back through the scrim so that the hidden point appears 25 mm to the right of the place of entry (Fig. 90b). When you can see the eye of the needle, wrap the loop of twine once round the eye of the needle and pull the needle through downwards and tighten up the twine (Fig. 90c).

5 Insert the needle about 50 mm to the right (Fig. 90d) and repeat this stitch all round the seat.

It will probably be necessary to join on more twine, which is done by making a knot in the remaining end as closely as possible to the stuffing. Make another loose knot in the new

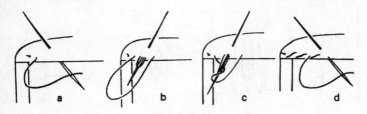

Figure 90

159

piece of twine and slip over the knot in the short end, pulling the new twine so that the loose knot tightens and the join is secure.

SECOND ROW OR TOP STITCHING

Before commencing further stitching, examine the stuffing by feeling with the fingers. Use a regulator to work up the edge. This is done by pushing the sharp end of the regulator into the scrim and gradually, with a raking action, pulling some of the stuffing towards the edge to make it firmer.

1 Secure the thread about 12 mm above the previous row of stitching.

2 Slope the needle as before but this time bring the needle right through (Fig. 91a).

3 Push the needle back into the scrim, eye-end first, and about 20 mm away from where it came out (Fig. 91b).

4 Twist the twine round the needle (Fig. 91c) and pull through.

5 Insert the needle about 50 mm to the right (Fig. 91d) and repeat.

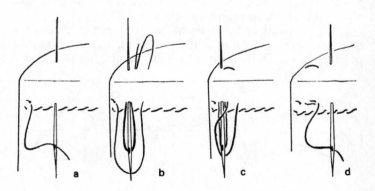

Figure 91

THIRD ROW OR TOP STITCHING

A third or fourth row is often required, but this depends upon the depth of the stuffing together with the firmness of the edge. In the making of easy chairs they should always be used.

SECOND STUFFING

Place a thin layer of fibre or hair on top of the hessian filling up the ditch formed by the stitching. Cover with a layer of wadding. Another method is to use thick upholstery wadding but make sure that the ditch is filled in. This can be done by a small strip of the wadding. 25 mm foam sheeting could also be used but be careful not to have bulk at the corners.

COVERING

Cut out a piece of calico large enough to cover the stool and sufficient to go underneath the frame for 50 mm. Centre the calico and knock in temporary tacks round the sides of the frame (Fig. 92a). Turn the frame upside down and tack the calico down on to the frame. Snip the calico down at each leg (Fig. 92b), and tack down to the frame, leaving the corners free. With the stool right way up cut the material up at the corners (Fig. 92c), turn under the raw edge of the side portion and tack to the front of the frame (Fig. 92d). Turn under the raw edge at the front of the cover and tack on (Fig. 92e).

A loose cover may be made to go over the calico – this has the advantage of being removable for washing. A fixed cover can be put on in the same way as the calico cover and the lower edge of the stool finished off with braid.

UNDERSIDE OF STOOL

Cut a piece of hessian the length of the stool plus 25 mm by the width plus 25 mm.

Turn under the raw edge and tack to the stool. Cut the hessian down at the corners (Fig. 92f), turn under the two edges and tack.

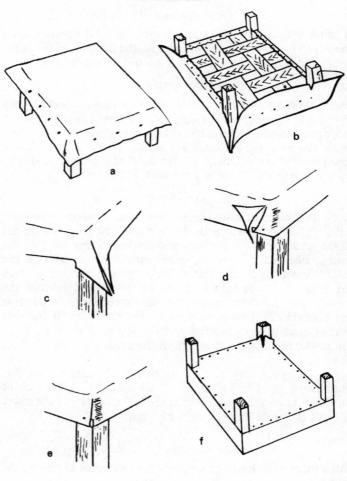

Figure 92

Pouffe

MATERIALS REQUIRED

Strong hessian or canvas.
Flock or rugging.
Foam sheeting to equal depth of pouffe and sufficient to go round sides.

METHOD

Cut out four circles of strong hessian about 460 mm in diameter and two strips of hessian 180 mm wide and 3½ times the diameter of the circle, plus 50 mm (approximately 1400 mm). Join the ends of side band together with a 20 mm seam. Fold the circle into four to mark the position of each quarter (Fig. 93a); divide the side band into quarters and join together (Fig. 93b). Attach the second circle to the side band in the same way but leave an opening. Turn right side out. Fill with stuffing to make solid, then stitch up opening (Fig. 93c). Make a second pad like this one and join the two together (Fig. 93d).

Wrap the piece of foam sheeting round the pouffe, stitch ends together, then tie a cord round to form a waist.

COVER

Make the outer cover in the same way as the pouffe, but tack round each circle carefully the depth of the turning from the edge. This is to prevent the circle being stretched out of shape. The side band should be the depth of the pouffe plus turnings, and is joined to the one circle (Fig. 93b). If a piping is required it should be attached to the circles or the side band. Place pouffe inside cover and attach second circle, using the markings as in Fig. 93a and b. Tie cord round waist of pouffe to give a good finish (Fig. 93e).

Loose covers could be made so that the pouffe fits in with the decor of a room. Two ideas are given in Fig. 93f and g.

163

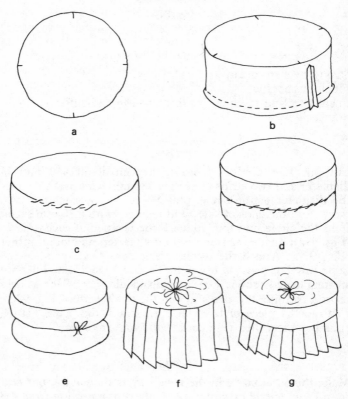

Figure 93

Latex foam upholstery

The use of various types of foam has made upholstery very much easier and speedier than the conventional form, although one may wish to continue using springs with the addition of foam; but foam can be used with rubberised webbing to give a good, soft but slightly sprung effect.

The real latex foam was orginally made from the rubber tree, but today it is supplemented with vast quantities of synthetic rubber. The most synthetic is polyether foam, which is widely used in upholstery. It is highly inflammable, but there is research going on to find ways of making it less dangerous in the home. It is wisest to buy the best quality of latex foam that one can afford for the best results.

TYPES OF LATEX FOAM

Plain sheeting (Fig. 94a) is obtainable in sheets approximately 1800 by 1370 mm and 15-25 mm thick. It can be used for 'drop in' or pincushion type seats; may also be used for arms of small chairs or doming (i.e. building up of layers of various sizes) when a firm, rounded seat is required.

Pin-core foam (Fig. 94b). This type of foam has approximately 5 mm diameter cavities which pass right through the foam. Cushions made from this type of foam are reversible. When using this foam for upholstery, it is necessary to use a layer of wadding or thin polyether foam and then a layer of calico before putting on the final cover. This is to prevent shadows of the holes in the foam showing after the furniture has been in use for a short period.

Cavity sheeting (Fig. 94c) is obtainable in sheets approximately 200 by 150 mm and varying in thickness from 50 to 100 mm. This type of foam sheeting has a smooth skin on one side and cavities on the reverse. If the skin is very thin and the cavities are large then the upholstery will not retain its shape and stability for a long time. This type of foam requires walling if a square edge is required – see page 170.

Moulded units (Fig. 94d). These are available in various shapes and sizes. There is a continuous skin from the top, forming solid walls. These are non-reversible, but two pads can be joined together with adhesive to form a reversible pad (Fig. 94e). The two cavities must be facing.

Note: When foam, especially latex, is left exposed to the light over a prolonged period, the surface will discolour and start to crumble. This is why an undercover is used on cushions.

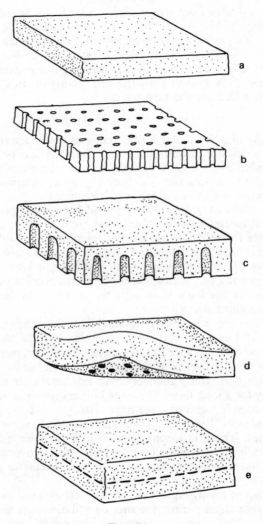

Figure 94

166

Foam will shape easily to the requirements of the up-holsterer providing it is dealt with in certain ways. For rounded edges a form of feathering may be carried out, but at all times calico should be attached to the foam to enable it to be held in place on the wooden frame of the furniture.

FEATHERING

1 When using 25 mm sheeting, cut the foam 10 mm larger than the base. The extra 10 mm is tapered off to half the depth of the foam. A strip of calico 40-50 mm wide is attached to the top edge only, a depth of 15-20 mm is stuck to the upper edge of the foam (Fig. 95a).

2 Feathering to a point is used for upholstering pin-cushion seats or back insets. The foam is again cut slightly larger, about 10 mm. It is then feathered to an angle of 30° right to the top edge and then calico is attached to the top edge as before, and also to the cut edge. The two pieces of calico are treated as one when attaching to the frame (Fig. 95b).

3 Shaped Edge (pin-core). Again, cut the foam 10-15 mm larger, but this time taper the edge to within 10 mm of the top edge (Fig. 95c). Attach the calico (Fig. 95d) and tack to the underside of the frame (Fig. 95e).

4 Cushioned Edge. This is used when a steeper and firmer edge is required. The foam is cut 10-25 mm wider than the frame and the calico is attached (Fig. 95f). The calico is then tacked to the frame, any surplus foam being tucked under in the process.

Note: It is essential that the edge of the foam is always perfectly straight before the calico is attached because the tacks go through the calico just below the edge of the foam.

5 Square Edge. This gives an attractive tailored effect if a piped edge is used on the cover, and is most commonly used on stools and some types of chairs which have no arms.

If using solid foam or pin-core, cut the foam slightly larger than the base. Attach a strip of calico, which is then tacked to the frame (Fig. 96a). The outer cover should be the same size

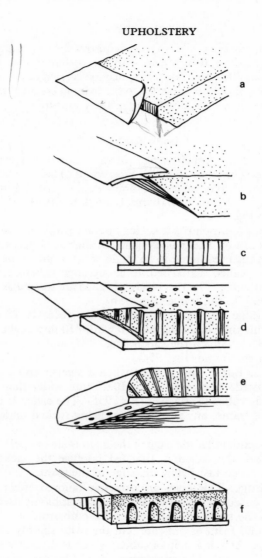

Figure 95

168

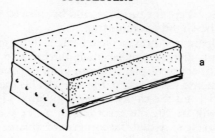

a

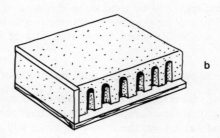

b

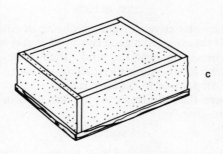

c

Figure 96

as the base, except for turnings, and because of the tight fit the foam will be slightly compressed.

Cavity foam requires a boxed edge. This means that the foam is cut slightly smaller than the base to allow for the walling. Cut strips of plain 10 mm foam to equal the depth of cavity foam and the length of the sides. (This means that it will protrude beyond the cavity foam, Fig. 96b). The two remaining sides will be cut the exact length of the foam (Fig. 96c). This is to make sure that the corners are square. It is all held in place with adhesive. Calico is attached to each side as in Fig. 96a.

If the walling is to be used on a shaped seat, e.g. an oval stool, then it may be possible to cut one continuous strip, but this must not be stretched when attaching to the pad (pincore).

The repairing of chairs with loose lift-off seats

This type of seat is usually used for dining-room chairs and for a large variety of stools, especially those covered with tapestry. After considerable wear the seat of the chair will sag, and upon inspection of the underside it will probably be found that the webbing has broken.

TO REPAIR

Remove the outer cover carefully by using the mallet and tack remover. If the cover is in good condition it may be used again.

Next remove the wadding and calico cover and cut any stitching which is holding the stuffing in place. Take out the tacks and strip down to the bare frame.

Make sure that the frame of the seat is firm and if at all insecure, re-glue.

METHOD

1 Place three strips of webbing across the frame each way (Fig. 84). Do not drive the tacks into the old holes, otherwise the webbing will not be firm.
2 Cut a piece of hessian the size of the seat plus 20 mm

turnings on all sides. Turn the 20 mm turnings on to the upper side of the seat and drive in the tacks (Fig. 84).

3   Cut a piece of 25 mm thick plain foam the size of the seat, feather the sides and attach calico to the edge (Fig. 95a). Place foam on to the seat and tack to underside of seat, taking care to centre each side (i.e. marking the half-way position of the length of each side, both of foam and seat base).

4   Place the outer cover on again marking each side as before. Make two pleats at the corners, both facing towards each other (Fig. 97b). Place in two temporary tacks, which can be removed after tacking the cover to the underside.

Note: If the old cover is of real leather and in good condition it should be damped evenly all over and pinned to a large board and stretched. When it is dry, re-polish it and put back on to the chair. If tapestry was used it should be dry-cleaned.

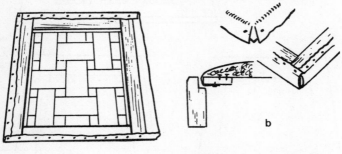

a   Figure 97

Stool with drop-in seat

This is made the same as the chair seat, but if it is large a domed effect may be required. For a large open area place the webbing 40-50 mm apart.

Cut the foam (25 mm thick) 10 mm larger all round than the frame. Use 10 mm thick sheeting for the dome and this should be 40-50 mm smaller all round than the thicker foam. Stick the two pieces together at the corners. Feather the larger piece and make up as for chair seat.

171

Pin cushion seat (renewing) (Fig. 98a)

Usually the seat requires repairing because of broken webbing. The outer cover of the seat may be in good condition and can be used again. Strip down the chair seat to the framework.

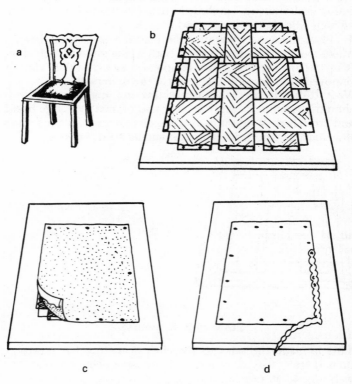

Figure 98

METHOD

1 Attach three strips of webbing each way (Fig. 98b) using a webbing stretcher (Fig. 81).

2   Measure from the back to the front of the seat plus 25 mm and from side to side plus 25 mm, and cut out a piece of hessian straight by the thread.

3   Mark the centre of the seat and the centre back. Fold the hessian into two and crease. Place the crease to the centre front and centre back of the seat. Fold up 10 mm turning and knock in a tack on the front edge, and then the back, and continue tacking the hessian on to the seat (Fig. 98c).

4   Cut a piece of 25 mm thick foam sheeting the size of the open area plus 10 mm on each side. Feather these sides (Fig. 95a) and attach calico. Turn under edge of calico and tack into position on the fold of calico (Fig. 98c).

5   Replace the outer cover which will have the raw edges showing and then cover this edge with a gimp, using gimp pins. If leather is used, use a leather gimp and studs.

Padded box (Fig. 99a)

There may be an old upholstered box which was used for blankets, toys, etc. and is now shabby. Remove the lid and put the hinges and screws in a safe place. Strip down both the box and lid and check that they are still sound. If any joints need making secure strengthen them at this stage. The lid may then be padded.

METHOD

1   Cut a piece of 50 mm thick foam sheeting or pin-core the size of the lid, plus 15 mm on all sides. Feather the sides to within 15 mm of top edge (Fig. 95a). If the lid is large and a slightly domed effect is required, for this use a piece of 15-25 mm plain sheeting; cut it 50 mm smaller all round and place adhesive on the corners of both the sheeting and the base, then join together (Fig. 99c). This should be done prior to feathering.

2   Tear strips of calico 70 mm wide and equal in length to the sides plus 100 mm on each piece. Mark a 40 mm border on top of the foam (unfeathered side). Spread this area thinly with

173

adhesive. Mark a 30 mm border on each strip of calico and spread this also with adhesive. (Keep flat, edges must not roll.) When adhesive is tacky (dull) place the calico on to the foam just below the 40 mm border marking (Fig. 99b). Repeat this for all sides (Fig. 99d).

3 Mark the mid-point of each side of the lid, also that of the calico. Place the foam flat on a table with feathered side uppermost then place the lid on top, matching the mid-points (Fig. 99e).

4 Bring down top edge of calico on long side and place in temporary tacks. Make sure that the foam does not come over the edge of wood (Fig. 99f). Then bring over the calico on the other long side and place in temporary tacks, again being careful not to allow foam to come over the wood. Snip the calico at the end of lid (Fig. 99f), and lift that piece of calico up to reveal foam. Bring back as in Fig. 99g and tack to lid, trim off any surplus calico. Repeat for all corners.

5 Bring the short side pieces of calico over and tack, working from the mid-point of each side towards the corners. Cut the calico as for Fig. 99f at the corners and open out. Pull gently at an angle of approximately 45° (Fig. 99h), mark with a pencil, then put adhesive on both pieces and join together. Take the end of calico to underside of lid and hold in place with a couple of tacks. Remove surplus fabric.

Note: All temporary tacks can be driven home if the calico and foam fit satisfactorily.

UNDERCOVER AND TOP COVER

1 If using pin-core foam, cut a piece of wadding to cover the padded area of the lid. Cover with calico and secure at the mid-point of each long side to the underside of the lid with temporary tacks.

2 Make sure that the grain of fabric is parallel to the side of the lid before tacking along one side to within 70 mm of the corner.

174

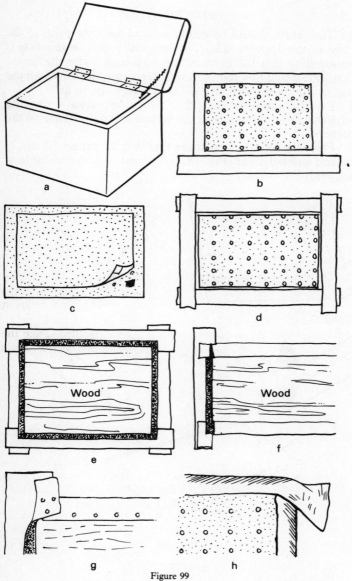

Figure 99

3 The fabric should be gently stroked with the palm of the hand to the opposite side. The temporary tack on this side is removed so that the foam can be tightened under the cover. Continue doing this and putting in temporary tacks. When the whole is smooth (no wrinkles) then secure the tacks.

4 Do the same to the other two sides, always stroking outwards from the centre of the lid and to within 70 mm of the corners.

5 Place the top cover on (make sure that the pattern, if any, is central and balanced (Fig. 18, p. 20) and tack to underside of lid, omitting corners (Fig. 100a).

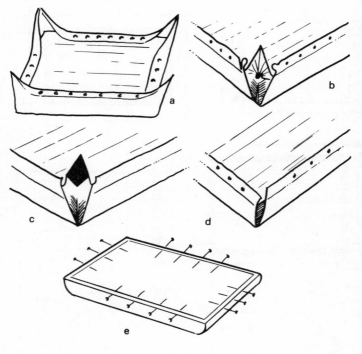

Figure 100

6   Holding the calico and cover together, pull upwards and away from the corner towards the underside of the lid and put in a tack (Fig. 100b). Cut away the surplus (Fig. 100c) and make a fold in the fabric so that the fold is parallel to the edge of the corner (Fig. 100d). Crease well and trim off any surplus fabric before finally tacking down.

7   Cut a piece of fabric to line the lid, allowing 10-15 mm for turnings. Turn under raw edge and pin (Fig. 100e). Hem to the outer cover. Before finally stitching mark on the lid the position of the hinges.

COVERING OF BOX

1   Cover the sides of the box with wadding. This should be of the exact depth of the box and sufficient to go all the way round without overlapping. Have the join of wadding at one corner and place tacks in temporarily to hold it in place (Fig. 101a). The wadding is used to prevent the outer cover wearing against the hard corners of the wood. Foam sheeting 10 mm thick may be used instead of wadding.

2   Cut the outer cover the depth of the box plus 90 mm. If the material is not wide enough to go all the way round the box place any joins at the corners.

3   Place the material round the sides of the box. Allow 50 mm to tuck inside the box and 25 mm to go underneath.

4   To join the material on the side of the box, turn the two raw edges in away from each other and oversew together as in Fig. 101b. If you have a 40 mm curved needle this may be used and the join can then be slip-stitched.

5   Tack the material to the inside of the box and under side.

6   Cover the bottom of the box with hessian (this must be cut by a straight thread (Fig. 101c). Tack all round.

INSIDE OF BOX

1   Cut pieces of cardboard the exact size of each side, ends and bottom of the box.

177

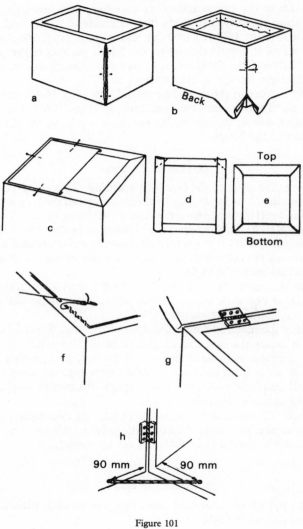

Figure 101

2 Cut the material for lining 25 mm larger all round than the pieces of cardboard.

3 Place the cardboard in the centre of the material on the wrong side and stick the two sides of material to the cardboard (Fig. 101d).

4 Cut away the surplus material; the dotted line indicates where the material should be cut. Fold down the raw edges and stick to the cardboard on all four sides (Fig. 101e).

5 Place the side pieces of cardboard into the box and hem to the top edge (Fig. 101f).

6 Place the bottom piece of cardboard into the box. This should be a tight fit.

ATTACHING THE LID

1 Place the hinges on to the lid (Fig. 101g) about 85 mm from the end. Make the holes with a gimlet, then insert the screws.

2 Place the lid on to the box and fix the hinges in the same way.

3 To support the lid of the box when it is open, use a length of chain and measure 90 mm from the ends of the box and secure the chain with screws (Fig. 101h).

Re-webbing of sprung seat (Fig. 102)

Broken webbing may cause the seat of a chair to sag and be uncomfortable to sit on. It can be easily repaired.

Turn the chair upside down and remove the hessian or linen which covers the webbing by using a ripping chisel and a mallet (Fig. 80). Untie the springs from the broken webbing and remove one of the broken pieces. Interlace with new webbing and secure (Fig. 85). The tacks must not be placed in holes previously made. Renew all broken webbing in the same way. Stitch the springs to the webbing, using a spring needle and thick twine. Cover with new hessian as in Fig. 92f.

ALTERNATIVE METHOD

Remove all the broken webbing from the chair. The springs will then appear to shoot upward and should be lashed down to

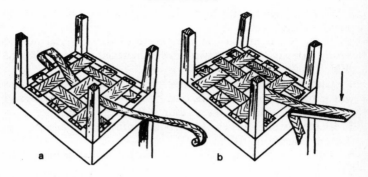

Figure 102

the frame with laid cord (Fig. 85e), tying the first coil of every spring securely. Then re-web the complete seat and cover with hessian or linen.

Re-seating of an easy chair (Fig. 103)

The seat is the first part of a chair to show signs of wear. It becomes uncomfortable to sit upon and probably a new seat is required.

STRIPPING DOWN

Turn the chair upside down, resting the seat upon a stool or box. Remove the hessian and webbing which is attached to the bottom of the chair by knocking out the tacks with a ripping chisel and mallet (Fig. 80). Take out the tacks which hold the back cover and outside arms to the seat rails. Pin back these portions of the cover, thus giving access to the seat. Remove all tacks, holding any portion of the seat to the frame. The chair should appear as in Fig. 103.

RE-SEATING

1 Place about five strands of webbing across in each direction and attach as in Fig. 84c. Turn the chair right side up. From

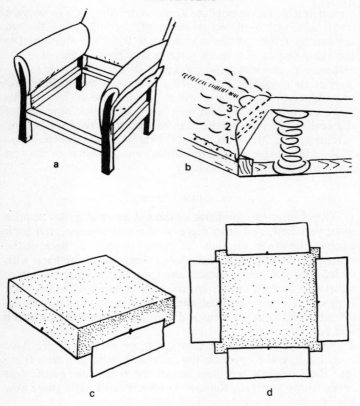

Figure 103

the old seat, which has already been removed, take out the springs. Note their previous position. If any are broken replace with new ones. Stitch the springs to the webbing (Fig. 85). They should be in a position similar to that in the old seat.

2   Lash the springs down (Fig. 85e), the front, back and side

181

ones being tied at an outward angle so that they will be straight when a weight is placed on the centre spring. Place the old hessian over the springs to make sure that they are lashed to the same height. Cut out a piece of new hessian the same size and attach, and stitch the springs to it (Fig. 87).

3 Put in the bridles (Fig. 88), pick over the stuffing and re-stuff. Cut out a piece of scrim the same size as the previous piece and attach to the seat rail. Stitch along the front edge of the seat with blind stitch (Fig. 90) and then two rows of top stitching (Fig. 91). A section of the three rows is shown in Fig. 103b. Make three rows of bridles across the centre of the seat and stuff; cover with wadding.

COVERING OF SEAT

1 Check over the condition of the old cover as it may require to be repaired, and then place on the seat, pushing the back edge of the cover through the space between the back of the chair and the seat and attach to the seat rail at the back with tacks. Pull the cover towards the front of the chair and place temporary tacks 50 mm from the edge of the cover to the front edge of the chair rail. Push the sides of the cover through the openings between the arms and seat, pull down and tack to the seat rail.

2 Turn the chair upside down, remove the pins which have been holding the cover on the arms and back, and tack these into their original position. Secure the front edge of the seat cover to the seat rail. Remove temporary tacks and place new hessian over the webbing (Fig. 92f).

RE-SEATING USING FOAM

Use Pirelli webbing (no springs required) and stretch the webbing to ⅞ its length and attach to upper frame of the seat.

1 Use a piece of 100 mm deep foam, equal in size to the chair seat, plus 100 mm on each side. If 100 mm is not available then use two pieces of 50 mm and join together with adhesive. Tear strips of calico 70 mm deep and equal to the width of the chair

between the legs. Mark the middle of each strip, also the foam, and attach calico to the lower 25 mm of foam (Fig. 103c).

2   Place the foam on to the webbing and pull the calico strips through the frame to the outside and hold in place with tacks 70 mm apart.

3   To dome the seat use a piece of 30 mm foam the exact size of the seat. Feather to a point (Fig. 95b) on all four sides. Place on to the seat and make sure it is central, then apply adhesive to the four corners.

4   Using a piece of 50 mm foam, which is the size of the seat plus 180 mm extra on each side, tear four pieces of calico the same as before, but 230 mm in depth. Mark the middle of the strips, also the foam, on the top side and attach calico to foam to a depth of 25 mm (Fig. 103d).

5   Place the foam over the doming and push the calico between the previous foam and the frame of the chair. Tack into position. The foam should be rolled at the front to give a cushioned edge.

Stool with foam seat (square-edged)

The stool is covered in the same way as a box lid, but if a square edge is required and pin-core foam is used then walling is necessary, as on pp. 169–70, Fig. 96b and c, and it is made slightly larger than the base. Attach strips of calico to the lower edge of the foam (this is the part attached to the stool frame). Make the top cover like a boxed cushion with a piped edge. A calico cover should be used with a pin-core foam.

Gimps and braids

Gimps and braids are extensively used to hide seams and finish the lower edges of stools or chairs.

On hide, use leather gimp and dome-headed nails (Fig. 104a) or leather-covered studs (Fig. 104b).

On cotton gimp and braid use gimp pins which can be purchased in the colour of the braid (Fig. 104c).

ATTACHING OF COTTON GIMP

Bind the end of gimp with cotton to prevent it coming undone (Fig. 104d) and turn this end under and secure to the back of a

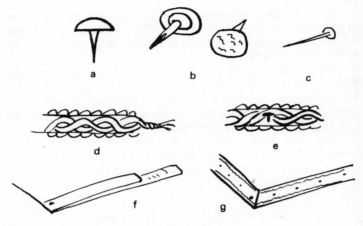

Figure 104

chair with a gimp pin. To attach the gimp to the chair, lift up part of the scroll and place a gimp pin underneath; drive it in and continue to do the same every two or three inches (Fig. 104e). Finish off by binding the gimp, folding underneath and securing with a gimp pin.

ATTACHING OF BRAID

A row of matching gimp pins is placed down the centre of the braid. If the braid is loosely woven, attach by stitching.

TO MITRE A CORNER

Fold back the braid at the corner and put in a gimp pin near the fold (Fig. 104f). Turn corner and continue attaching the braid with gimp pins (Fig. 104g).

Staining and polishing

Note: All renovation of woodwork should be carried out while the frame is stripped, and before reupholstering.

PREPARATION OF WOOD SURFACE

To obtain a good finish to any wood the surface must first be prepared by smoothing over with glasspaper. The paper is best wrapped around a cork rubber or flat piece of wood to ensure an even pressure by rubbing with a flat surface. Always rub with the grain. Commence with a No. 3 or 4 (grit 70) glasspaper and finish with a No. 1 (grit 150).

To smooth the crevices of stool legs etc. it will be easier to rub very lightly with steel wool.

PLASTIC WOOD

Plastic wood can be purchased in tubes and tins and is used for filling in holes on the wood surface. It is similar to soft clay and is pressed into holes and crevices. It should be left slightly dome-shaped as the plastic wood shrinks when it dries. Leave for about 24 hours before attempting to level off and smooth.

STAINS

There are many varieties of prepared stains on the market. One of the best is called a wood dye, which is easy to apply and gives an even finish. Try the colour of the dye or stain on a spare piece of wood matching the surface to be dyed.

APPLYING OF STAIN

Apply the stain with a brush about 25-40 mm bristle for stools. Have the brush fairly wet, but not dripping. The work should be done quickly, applying the stain in the direction of the grain, beginning at the top edge and working down. Do not allow any edges to become dry before applying stain to the adjoining surface, otherwise a streak may form.

Note: It is usually found that the grain of the wood has been raised with the applying of the stain; smooth over again with fine glasspaper and dust down.

POLISHING

A liquid polish can be easily made by allowing 6-7 oz of bleached shellac crystals to 1 pint of methylated spirits; this forms a white polish, i.e. it does not darken the surface of the wood. A slightly coloured polish can be made from 4-6 oz of ordinary shellac crystals to 1 pint of methylated spirits. Place the crystals and methylated spirits in a clear bottle with a cork or screw top. The crystals take a few days to dissolve; if the bottle is shaken occasionally the crystals will dissolve more quickly.

If there is any difficulty in removing the cork or screw top of the bottle place the neck of the bottle under a tap of running warm water, which will help to free the cork.

BRUSH POLISH

Use a camel-hair mop (a No. 6). Pour a small quantity of the polish into a screw-top jar. A hole may be made in the lid and the handle of the brush pushed partly through the hole and secured to the lid by adhesive tape.

APPLYING OF POLISH BY BRUSH

Apply the polish with a brush, first lightly wiping any surplus polish from the brush by squeezing gently on the sides of the jar. Brush over very quickly, taking care not to leave any surface without polish; leave for several hours to harden.

APPLYING OF POLISH BY PAD

A further application of polish is made by a pad of soft cotton material, free of starch or dressing, into which a piece of wadding is placed. Pour on to the wadding a small quantity of polish, pull the material tight, and apply the lower edge of the pad to the surface of the wood. Work with a circular movement and do not press heavily at first, otherwise the polish will come through the pad too quickly. It is not the quantity of polish which makes for a good surface but the pressure in applying and moving the pad. When the pad becomes very sticky, apply a drop of linseed oil to the pad. This makes it move more freely. To obtain a high polish many applications of polish will be required.

To keep the rubber pad soft when not in use, place in an air-tight container.

WAX POLISHES

Wax polish is made from beeswax mixed with a little turpentine to make it soft, preferably pure American turpentine. Shred the beeswax into a tin and partly cover with turpentine. Place the tin in a pan of hot water reaching half-way up the sides of the tin. The pan may be placed on a low heat, as heat helps the wax to dissolve. For very light work use bleached beeswax and turpentine.

APPLYING OF POLISH

A wax polish should be applied to a surface with a soft rag and left for 24 hours, so that the turpentine will evaporate. Afterwards remove all trace of the wax by rubbing hard with a soft cloth.

NATURAL OAK

There are times when a light finish is required. To obtain this do not apply any stain to the surface of the wood. Commence by using a white liquid polish and afterwards rub with a white wax polish.

Tension or cable springs

This type of spring is used a great deal for fireside chairs together with latex foam cushions. It differs from the ordinary spring which contracts when weight is applied, as it expands under pressure.

RENEWING OF SPRINGS

There are several methods of attaching these springs. On careful inspection of the chair it will be found that they are attached by one of the following methods:

(a) hooked into metal strips attached to the framework (Fig. 105a);

(b) hooked into small hooks secured into the frame (Fig. 105b);

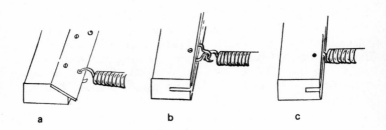

a   b   c

Figure 105

(c) hooked into a groove in the frame and secured by a nail or screw (Fig. 105c).

To renew the springs in (a) and (b), unhook the old spring and replace with a new one. To replace the spring in (c) remove the nail and spring; insert the new spring and nail.

TO CONVERT CHAIR TO TENSION SPRINGS

This can be done if the woodwork is in good condition. The rails of the seat must not be too low down; when using tension springs with latex foam cushions the total depth of the seat will be 130 mm. When using ordinary springs and stuffing the total depth may be 180-260 mm. Therefore, by using tension springs you are actually reducing the height of the chair from the floor. With this type of springing the framework of the chair is seen. If the wood is in good condition it may be stained and polished or covered with fabric to match the cushion.

The springs may be attached by any one of the previous methods, but (b) is the simplest way. These springs stretch from side to side of the chair and are spaced about 80-130 mm apart.

Useful addresses

Springs Hoover Ball & Bearing Co (UK) Ltd, 55 Progress Road, Eastwood, Industrial Estate, LEIGH-on-SEA, Essex SS9 5JJ

Webbing Barnes and Co. Materials Ltd, 1 Torridon Road, Hither Green, LONDON SE13 6TD

Barnes (Manchester) Ltd, Lansdale Street, Walkden, MANCHESTER M28 5GN

F. Drake & Co. (Webbing) Ltd, North Coker Mills, EAST COKER, Somerset

Upholstery frames H. Vaughan Ltd, 26 Naval Row, LONDON E14 9PS

Mount Vernon Cabinet Works, 61 Mason Street, LIVERPOOL 7

Fletcher, Mayfield & Co. Ltd, Arterial Road, Eastwood, LEIGH-on-SEA, Essex

Wadding Cotton Felt Products Ltd, Livesey Street Mill, Elton, BURY

D. L. Forster Ltd, 17 Tramway Avenue, Stretford, LONDON E15 4PG

Robert Hamilton Ltd, Birchinlee Mill, Royton, Nr OLDHAM OL2 5ER

Harbour Lane Mill Co. Ltd, Drury Lane, Hollingwood, OLDHAM

Foam cushions The National Rubber Research Ass., 19 Buckingham Street, Adelphi, LONDON WC2

Latex Cushion Co., Birmingham Ltd, 830 Kingsbury Road, Erdington, BIRMINGHAM 24

General The Russell Trading Co. Ltd, 75 Paradise Street, LIVERPOOL L13 BP for chair frames, stool pads, boxes, ottomans and all general requisites for upholstery (suppliers to schools)

Braids, gimps and cords Distinctive Trimmings Co. Ltd, 17d Kensington Church Street, LONDON w8

Index